Advance Praise for
Dance into Your Power

"A gripping read. Maia builds instant rapport and connection as she shares her own journey as an authentic inspiration to others. She's living proof of the resilience of the human spirit and the ability to extract lessons from a troubled and challenging start in life. In this book, Maia creates a clear road map for others and engages the reader every step of the way regardless of age, gender or life experience. "

—Kate Burton, PCC
International Coach and Author of *Live Life. Love Work*, *Coaching with NLP for Dummies*, and *NLP for Dummies*

"Reading *Dance into Your Power* felt as though Maia had written this book just for me—it was like having a conversation with her. It is my personal and professional experience that dancing brings a rare kind of joy and peace into your life and Maia has beautifully connected that to her road map for developing your powerful presence.

Dance is powerful. We are powerful. Dancing through life's challenges is easier than you think—and Maia will show you how! If you are looking for realistic and comforting inspiration, keep reading. I hope you dance, too."

—Jennifer McDonald
Owner/Director, Martell School of Dance

"Maia Beatty is the embodiment of Powerful Presence and her completely authentic, no holds barred, fully alive spirit jumps off the pages of this book. She offers her readers a clear, simple roadmap based on her own life experience for dancing into their own authentic power."

—Cathy Jacob, CPCC, Partner
Fire Inside Leadership Coaching

i

"Once I started reading this book, I couldn't stop! Maia is such a talented writer. I think it's amazing that she shared her personal story, I learned so much about her. What an adventure! And what a wonderful gift to give people: the keys to their own personal power. This book is perfect for anyone who wants to discover their personal power and experience the confidence and peace that comes from that."

—Stephanie Ward
The Marketing Coach for Entrepreneurs
Firefly Coaching

"Maia's story will pull your heart right out of your chest and make you want to run instead of walk towards your passion in life. After reading this book, I've felt more compelled than ever to connect with my inner self and harness the power within to turn my dreams into reality. This book is a must-read! "

—Zipporah Groth, CLTC, CLU®, ChFC®, CASL
Financial Advisor

"As someone who strives to continually grow and evolve I'm thrilled to have been introduced to Maia's latest book, *Dance into Your Power*. What an amazing and unusual journey Maia's life has been! I believe the resulting wisdom and processes gleaned from her journey is exactly where a treasure lies for all of us as we continue upon ours.

Maia teaches you how to "identify, claim, and access your own personal power" so you can soar unlimited as you create your future. If you're like me, always hungry for growth and to thrive on all levels of life, then this book is one you will delight in!"

—Loree Bischoff, Life Coach
Author of *Common Sense Happiness*

"This is a wonderful book! Maia has transformed her incredible story into a resource that's emotional, compelling and inspirational. Her writing is deceptively easy to read, while being profound and unconventional at the same time. I've come away from it with many golden nuggets that will benefit me and my clients for years. This book is a must read!"

—Kate Franklin, CPCC, MCIPD
Director, Oak Tree Coaching Ltd.

Dance into Your Power is a gift. Maia tells an extraordinary tale born from her own life experiences and trials, and the message and intention behind it is not only clear to understand, but also inspiring and more importantly, powerfully motivating. You will want to keep reading, and beyond that—begin to dance from your own set of instincts and transform your life. The concept here is immeasurably exciting."

—Tara Tober, Artistic Director,
Contact Dance Academy

"Maia Beatty is an amazing coach and trainer, and she shares her personal story and innovative strategies in a way that is accessible to everyone. *Dance into Your Power* will take you on an inspirational and enlightening journey to find your own Powerful Presence. I highly recommend this book."

—Heather Steranka-Petit
Global Diversity Consultant

"In *Dance into Your Power*, Maia Beatty clearly demonstrates that despite negative childhood and adult experiences you can take charge of your own destiny joyously. My advice is to let this inspirational read show you how to do it for yourself. I highly recommend this book."

—Rose Pellar, Barrister and Solicitor
Author of *A Gift in Every Challenge*

"Reading Maia's book has changed my awareness of how I work with my patients. Her exploration of the dynamics of Powerful Presence has illuminated for me the dance we do as doctors and patients during every office visit, even though I've been doing it for over 30 years. *Dance into Your Power* solidified for me the idea I've had that, in order for true healing to occur, the music we bring to this dance must come from our hearts, not just our minds. This is a powerful book that I highly recommend."

—Dr. Kenneth J. Klak, D.O.

"Dance into Your Power is chock-full of wonderful insights, clear inspiration and practical strategies useful for anyone looking to reclaim, or boost, their personal power. It has my highest recommendation."

—Deirdre McEachern
Master-Certified Career and Life Coach
Author of *You Only Live Once: Create the Life You Want*

"*Dance into Your Power* invites you into one woman's life where you will learn valuable life lessons that will help you every day. Maia's positive message and the "distinctions, structures, and strategies" she shares in this book will inspire you to dance in ways that will transform your life!"

—Lori Maloney Young
Planner, Facilitator, Trainer, Advocate, Mother

"This book is superb! Maia is clearly a fully present, positive and very balanced person, so I was both surprised and deeply touched by the very painful experiences she lived through, learned from and transformed in her life. She shows you exactly how she has healed her life and moved on to be the amazing woman she is today, and she gives you a road map that anyone can follow! Maia shares with you everything you need to know to join her in creating a life that is more joyful, connected and lived with greater ease."

—Betsy Muller, Speaker and Coach
Best-selling Author of *Energy Makeover*

Also by
Maia Beatty

Bootstrap Words: Pull Yourself UP! (1995)

Pizza and the Art of Life Management (1996)

The Trainer's Cookbook: Designing Learner-focused, Performance-based Training (2004)

The Traveler's Pocket Guide to the Journey to Powerful Presence (2012)

Dance into your POWER

A Woman's Journey to Powerful Presence

Maia Beatty

Love Your Life

Love Your Life

Love Your Life Publishing
www.loveyourlifepublishing.com

ISBN: 978-1-934509-58-6
Library of Congress Control Number: 2012947496

Printed in the United States of America

First Printing 2012

Editing by Gwen Hoffnagle

Cover design and layout by Chuck Beatty
www.reflectionsonnature.com

Back cover photo by Toby Shingleton, TKPhotography
www.tobyshingleton.com

*For Gwen Nichols, who showed me the path to my Journey
and gave me the tools to begin it.*

*For all of the Dancers who have joined me on
The Journey to Powerful Presence
in my classes and teleclasses since September of 2009
and you—who join us in the Dance.*

*For my sister, Susan Rich,
whose presence on my Journey is a treasure.*

*And—as always—for my Darling Charlie,
who knows all the reasons why.*

Preface

This book is about power.

This is the kind of power that allows you to defeat any obstacle, overcome the most difficult odds and withstand the most oppressive circumstances.

It's the kind of power that creates heroes out of ordinary people. Stepping into power like this affects you at the deepest level. It transforms you—and everything around you.

If those five sentences caught your attention and you're still reading, then you are an extraordinary person. Talking about power is not something most of us do on a regular basis, if at all. Power is not a word that most people would say in the same sentence as their name. Yet power is the one thing that allows you to fulfill your own destiny and create a joyfully successful life.

How would you like to have the power to simply be yourself and live your life by playing to your strengths, no matter what anyone else says or does?

How would you like to be able to say no when you want to, and say yes to the things you choose for yourself, on your timeline, in your own way?

How would you like to be able to defy the limitations placed on you by society because of your gender, your age, your culture, or anything else about you, and achieve anything you dream of doing?

The power to do that—and more—is at your fingertips. You just have to know how to find it.

Searching for this power has taken me on a forty-year Journey from seventeen-year-old runaway with nothing but the clothes on my back and $30 in my pocket, through years of dead ends and defeats, to discovering and harnessing it at its source. Over the last twenty years, I've been sharing my strategies with thousands of people all over the globe. Along the way, this power has given me a life of fulfillment and success, both personally and professionally.

If you want to discover and harness this power for yourself, this book will give you a proven blueprint—and it will take you a fraction of the time it took me, since everything you need is at your fingertips.

Even though the secret is right here in your hands, you have to add the special ingredients to make it your own: your time and your attention. This is true for all great power.

Remember Dorothy's ruby slippers in The Wizard of Oz? Remember the end of the movie when the Wizard has flown away in the balloon, and Dorothy fears that she'll never get back home? Then Glinda arrives and tells her that she has everything she needs to make her wish come true in the ruby slippers she's been wearing since she landed in Oz; that all she has to do to access their magic is to click her heels three times and speak her heart's desire. When Dorothy asks in exasperation, "Why didn't you just say so?!" Glinda replies, "You wouldn't have believed me!"

Believe me.

To get the full benefits of this power, you have to take your own Journey to it. You'll find the road map in this book, with everything you need to be successful—in your own time and in your own way. Although my Journey helped me create the map, the women (and some exceptional men) who have taken this Journey over the last several years have proven that every Journey is as unique as the person who takes it. Every Journey is a unique experience, whether it's your first time or your tenth.

As I traveled on my own Journey, there were times when I walked it. Other times I crawled or trudged or ran. I've climbed it and I've flown it. Then I learned to dance it.

Once I learned to dance my Journey, I discovered that a deep kind of joy happens when you move in this way. The more I learned to dance with everything I encountered on my Journey, the more powerful I became and the smoother the Journey became.

This is a book about power ... and I will show you how to dance!

Maia Beatty
Bath, Ohio
July 27, 2012

Dance into Your Power

Chapter Overview

Part One

Where It All Started

Dance into Your Power

Chapter 1

What is Powerful Presence?

Have you ever met somebody with whom you instantly connected? A moment before, she had been a complete stranger. Then she smiled at you and the whole room warmed up. All of a sudden, you felt like you were greeting an old friend for the first time. You felt seen and heard; you felt listened to and acknowledged, as if you were the only other person in the room. Most of all, you had the feeling that this person deserved your trust.

Here's what's so amazing about that: It can happen anywhere, even from across a crowded room. You could be at a meeting, you could be a member of an audience listening to a speaker, or part of a congregation listening to a sermon. It can happen one-on-one, when you're at the checkout counter at the grocery store, or returning books at the library. You could be getting into an elevator or finding your seat on a plane. You could be anywhere. That stranger could be anyone. Wherever and whenever it happens, you've just experienced Powerful Presence.

People with Powerful Presence are easy to spot because they have Three Resourceful Abilities in common. They:

1. Are conscious of their actions and their impact
2. Feel comfortable in their own skin
3. Know how to focus their Attention to get the most positive results

People with Powerful Presence come from all walks of life; they have their own personal styles and unique personalities. Even though they work in diverse arenas with a variety of professional skills, they all demonstrate these abilities.

People with Powerful Presence know something that others have not yet discovered: Your presence can only be experienced as your impact on other people. Everyone has a presence—it's up to you to make it powerful, since it comes from inside you. You can certainly make your presence powerful when you know where to start.

Powerful Presence has a structure.

> *Powerful Presence is the ability to act effectively*
> *in any situation in a way*
> *that inspires trust from other people.*

Powerful Presence can be learned.

When you're learning about Powerful Presence, it helps to start right at the beginning with the words themselves. When you look up the word *powerful* in the dictionary, you'll discover that it means "having or exerting power."

> *To have power means to have the ability or*
> *capacity to perform or act effectively.*

If you look up the word *presence*, you'll discover that it has several meanings:

1. the state of being present
2. a person's bearing, especially when it commands respectful attention
3. the quality of self-assurance and effectiveness that permits a performer to achieve rapport with an audience

All three of those statements describe the kind of presence we're talking about here. If you combine them with the definition of *powerful*, you get the truest description of the qualities of Powerful Presence:

1. the ability to live in—and communicate from—the present moment, including the ability to be conscious of the learning from your past and the desires of your future without staying stuck in either one
2. the kind of bearing that achieves respectful attention from others—as a direct result of the respectful attention one *gives* to others
3. the quality of self-assurance that results from being at home in your own skin; being able to create rapport with anyone you meet because you know, like, and trust yourself

> **When you master these three qualities,**
> **you become magnetic.**

Magnetic Behaviors

When you look a little closer, you'll see that people with Powerful Presence demonstrate seven specific behaviors that you can identify and measure. They are:

1. **Able to connect with you immediately**
   You instantly feel that you matter to them. It's clear that they're giving you their full attention; they're listening to you.

2. Attractive

You can sense their positive energy—no matter their age or their wardrobe. *Who they are being* draws you to them more powerfully than any fashion or style; you can feel they're happy with who they are.

3. Confident

You're clear they believe what they're saying, so it's easy for you to believe it, too. There is a marked absence of apologies or attempts to prove something.

4. Credible

It's evident they know what they're talking about; you can sense they have experience behind them. You get the feeling that their message is specifically for you; they listen to your needs and make their topic relevant to you.

5. Engaging

They're exceptional at asking questions, and they listen with interest to your answers. They're in conversation with you. Their ability to create dialogue with you makes it clear that your opinion is just as important to them as their own.

6. Flexible

They're adaptable; like a willow tree, they can bend in the strongest wind and bounce back from adversity. They're graceful, both physically and emotionally, so they can dance with whatever shows up. They dance to their strengths in ways that connect you to your own.

7. Inspirational

They have an impact. After being in their presence, you want to go out and take action. Being in conversation with them allows you to see your own strengths and possibilities.

How Do They Do It?

The ability to radiate Powerful Presence—that certain something that makes people's heads turn when you walk in the room—is more than your image. Powerful Presence is so simple it almost escapes your notice.

When you have Powerful Presence, you're being authentically you. With your attention focused appropriately, you're comfortable in your own skin and you're completely present.

Your ability to be present with another person—or a roomful or a stadium full of people—is the result of being able to focus your attention outside of yourself. That's easy to do when you know, like, and trust yourself. When you feel comfortable and confident, you don't have to keep checking in with yourself. That leaves you free to focus your attention on whomever you're with so you can connect with anyone and appreciate everything that's happening around you.

Being yourself—right here, right now—means that you've arrived without apologies or explanations, knowing you have nothing to prove. Other people can feel your confidence. You have danced into your power and you use your dancing to deepen your ability to know yourself, like yourself, and trust yourself. When you master that, you make it easy for others to know, like, and trust you, too.

If Powerful Presence is the ability to act effectively in any situation in a way that inspires trust from other people, what kind of impact do you think it will have on your ability to create the results you want in your life?

In the words of some of the graduates of the Journey to Powerful Presence, dancing into your power will allow you to:

- bring energy and focus back into your life
- create any level of success you desire
- develop better communication skills

- eliminate negativity from your life
- expand your creativity and self-confidence
- focus on possibilities instead of limitations
- increase the joy in your life
- realize your own power
- reduce your stress
- take any skill to the next level
- thrive in difficult situations
- work through obstacles with ease

These are the results that others have gotten by dancing into their power and developing their Powerful Presence. What about you? What would you like to achieve?

In the coming chapters, we'll explore the distinctions, structures, and strategies of the Journey to Powerful Presence so you can see how they work for you. This book is a road map that will help you develop your unique Powerful Presence through the use of:

- Three Empowering Beliefs
- Three Resourceful Abilities
- Three Focused Actions

The strategies you'll find in this book are the result of a Journey that took me almost forty years to complete. The good news is that I've synthesized what I discovered along the way into its most fundamental ingredients so you can take your own Journey in a fraction of that time.

Before you start your Journey, you may find it useful to see where mine began. Although my discoveries allowed me to create a magnetic presence that I tap in to daily, I assure you that this was not always the case.

The most exciting part of this Journey is that you can start from anywhere, with any level of confidence, and still develop behaviors that will transform your life. To see what I'm talking about, let's take a short trip to the past, to an autumn day in 1969 ...

Chapter 2

Every Journey Starts with the First Step

If you Google "October 15th, 1969," you'll find that this day marked the first National Moratorium to End the War in Vietnam. It was a historic day for me, too. It was the day that ended the active portion of the ongoing war my father and I had been waging against each other for over ten years, with my mother in the middle and my four sisters and my brother on the sidelines.

The impact of that first Moratorium was global; it began a process that eventually ended the war five years later. Another lesser-known impact of that first Moratorium was the hole in my family that took decades to address.

My involvement in the anti-war movement as a seventeen-year-old inspired me to resist all war, starting with the war in my home. It also set me on my path to the Journey to Powerful Presence, although I didn't know it at the time.

Childhood

In order to understand the significance of this particular October 15th, you have to understand the situation in which I grew up. As an Irish Catholic growing up in New York in the 1950s and '60s, I'd been raised to be obedient—I was just never very good at it. The war between my father and I developed, in part, because I never ceased questioning the status quo in our family; even as a child, I always thought there was more to the situation than I was being told. I had my own mind about things, too. If I couldn't get what I wanted directly, I found lots of ways to get it by alternate routes. These days you might call a child like this "creative." In those days I was described as "obstinate." It wasn't my intention to be obstinate—I was simply labeled that way when my father couldn't find a way to keep me obedient and docile.

When I was two years old, my mother had her first attack of multiple sclerosis after the birth of my second sister, Susan. With three babies under two years old, she certainly had an inordinate amount of stress. Her first attack occurred one evening as she was getting into her bath. We children were finally all asleep and she had a few precious moments to herself to relax in a hot bath. When she put her right foot in the water, she felt no heat; it was only when she put in her left foot that she realized that the water was scalding hot and she had no feeling in her right foot and leg.

The next day, she was taken to the hospital and my sisters Deirdre and Susan and I were sent to live with three different sets of relatives for the next six months. It took most of that time to arrive at her diagnosis, since MS wasn't as well known—or understood—as it is now.

When it came to being sent to relatives, I hit the jackpot. I went to live with my mother's parents, my Papa and Nanny. What a joy it was to be the center of their universe for those six months! I was the firstborn child of their only daughter, and, as far as they were concerned, the sun rose and set on my head. To this day, I believe that the love and nurturing I got from these two grandparents, combined with the nourishment I got from my mother in my first eleven months of life (before my sister, Deirdre—my *Irish twin*—was born) fueled a resilience deep inside me. No matter what happened to me, this solid foundation sustained me until I could finally dance into my own power.

Fast-forward to the return of all three children to our parents' home six months later. My father's life changed overnight. Not only did he have a wife whose illness required constant vigilance, he was suddenly the primary caretaker for three children under three years old. Adaptations to our lifestyle would have to be made. As a result, the world as we knew it changed again.

In his love for my mother, my father decided that her children were just too much for her. We must be kept quiet and obedient to give her the least amount of stress possible.

The love and attention we'd received from the relatives we'd just left was quickly replaced with behavior requirements that would support our two young parents in managing their children and keep my mother from having more MS attacks. We were quickly drilled in the requirement of strict obedience as we continued the separation from our mother that had begun six months earlier. You can imagine my two-and-a-half-year-old-self finding a way around all this structure, given the way I had experienced life up to this point! As a result, before I was three years old, my father and I began to be at odds.

In the process of keeping things quiet for my mother, my parents discovered a strategy that kept her MS symptoms at bay: pregnancy! Fifty years later, medical research would discover that the hormones of pregnancy reduce the symptoms of MS by up to 85 percent. In 1955, my parents were conducting their own research.

In the next five years, they had three more children. The first two pregnancies were wonderful for my mother and the births were relatively problem-free. But her last pregnancy almost killed her and the baby she carried; my youngest sister was delivered by C-section in February of 1962 as a seven-month preemie. Both of them had to stay in the hospital afterwards. My mother miscarried a seventh child before the year was out, then hemorrhaged daily for a year before finally submitting to a hysterectomy. After that, her health steadily deteriorated. Although she had periods of remission over the years, she was hospitalized on a regular basis for the rest of her life with a variety of autoimmune complications arising from her MS.

As a result of my mother's MS and the arrival of each new sibling, I was pushed into a role for which I was ill-suited: managing the chaos of a growing family without any knowledge or skill. As each new baby arrived and grew, the noise increased. According to my father, it was the responsibility of the oldest child to keep the others quiet and keep the peace. If there was a problem, it rested on the shoulders of the oldest child—me. I was often in trouble for failing to manage my job.

In the midst of his anger and frustration, the word he used to describe me in those days was "despicable!" Before I turned seven, I learned to read. One of the first things I did was look up that word. There, right in the dictionary, I could almost see it—a picture of my face, right next to the word. That's how I knew it was true about me.

This arrangement, and the knowledge of what I was, set me up to be separate from my siblings; how can you be one of them when you're in charge? Why would anyone want to be close to you if you're despicable? All of this removed me even further from my mother and put my father and me more deeply at odds. I needed him to love me and I hated him for how he treated me.

Before I was ten, there were six of us, each with our own needs for our parents' love and attention, and each with our own experience. Although it's clear to me at this distance that my parents did the very best they could under very trying circumstances, I remember feeling angry and isolated for much of my childhood.

It's also clear that I wasn't the only one feeling angry and isolated. Both my parents used prescription drugs to manage their feelings or their inability to sleep. The words *Valium* and *Librium* were familiar to me as a child and I took for granted that mixed drinks were a regular part of life.

As an adult, I discovered that there is alcoholism on both my mother's and father's sides of the family tree. In the early eighties, I was drawn to the newly formed association called Adult Children of Alcoholics, and was astounded to discover that there were other people in the world who felt and behaved exactly as I did, although that knowledge was years away from me as I was growing up.

School

My performance in school gave my father and me another opportunity to be at odds. Although I discovered in the mid-eighties that I have ADHD, there was no name for my style of learning when I was growing up. My ADHD provides me with huge benefits now; it's the reason I'm so good at creating strategies for everything, since I have to build my learning for myself from the inside out. As a result, I've become adept at teaching other people the "how" of things.

This was not the case as I was growing up. You can imagine how challenging it was for me to say what I needed in school—let alone for my parents or teachers to figure it out—when I didn't have the language or understanding that I have now. My family moved a lot, so when things got challenging for me I just figured I'd be in a new school the next year and gave up trying. As a result, if I didn't understand something in school and I had an unresponsive teacher, I'd just shut down. I wouldn't ask questions—I'd just get poor marks. This frustrated my parents immeasurably. Since each was brilliant academically with graduate degrees, they expected brilliance in their children. It must have been difficult for my PhD father to have a child with such a halfhearted attitude about school.

The stress of raising six children and caring for a spouse who was ill took its toll on my father. Although he mastered more domestic duties than many fathers of his generation—cooked dinner many nights, managed the groceries and the menus every month—he could become enraged at what seemed like the slightest provocation, often at dinner and always around the holidays. Although he often took us out to the beach or to play kickball at a nearby park so my mother could rest, he was quite handy with his belt and had no trouble whipping it off to deal with an errant child. Often that errant child was me. Although he read The Wind in the Willows to us when we were very small, with a different voice for every character, he could shout in your face or punch you with his fist, all in the name of keeping his children in line. Although these days we would call what he did "battering," in those days it was simply called "discipline."

As a child, I was unaware of his stresses; I only knew the impact he was having on me.

By the time I was twelve, I knew that I would leave home the moment I turned eighteen. There is a photo of our family taken during the summer of 1964 in which I'm standing apart from the group as if I'm not a part of the family—as if I've just stopped by to smile for the photographer. It's a snapshot of a family in turmoil, bravely trying to look good for the camera.

Runaway

Long before I was seventeen, I was doing my best to keep my head down and stay out of trouble at home. I was emotionally gone, whether I was immersed in a book, out with my friends, at my job, or writing my plans in my journal.

My fight with my father on October 15th, 1969, was over my boyfriend, a good young man from a warm and loving family who was wonderful to me and whom I loved. A few weeks earlier, after Ken and I had been together for about two years, my parents decided that we were getting too close, and I was forbidden to see him. Their directive was this: if either of my parents found out that we'd had any contact, I would be immediately taken out of school and there would be negative consequences for both of us.

On the day I left my home, this ongoing war between my father and me had come to a head. He was furious at me over something he imagined I had done, which I knew I hadn't. When he sent me to my room so he could confer with my mother about what to do with me, some part of me coolly decided that I had had enough.

So I grabbed the $30 I had from my past Saturday's pay envelope, wrote a farewell note to my parents, and walked out of the garage door with the clothes on my back. I had no idea where I would go or what I would do—I was simply leaving in protest over unjust parenting practices.

October 15th, 1969, was a day of protest all over this country. As I witnessed others of my generation engaging in civil disobedience to protest an unjust war that day, it gave me the idea that disobedience for a cause was a viable option. Believing I could disobey my parents for the sake of saving my own life gave me the nerve to walk out of their home that day.

The National Moratorium was a day that changed the world for me—as it changed it for everyone in my family. My actions had a tremendous impact on all of them that I only discovered many years later.

When I left home, I jumped out into my adulthood with a vengeance. I ran quickly away from everything I thought was the source of my misery into a world that was rapidly changing under my feet. My journey started with exhilaration.

As I started my new life, I was very lucky in three crucial ways. My boyfriend's mother had a friend who owned an apartment building with a three-room apartment for rent. Within two weeks it was mine—for $42 a month. My boss at the drug store where I worked adjusted my schedule to a full forty hours immediately, and I now earned $60 every week. So I had three things that made it easy for me to get on with my life: I had a home that was my own in a safe place, I had a job where I was valued, and I was out of the war zone of my family. Within a few months I completed the paperwork to be an "emancipated minor" in New York State, and I knew I was on my way.

When I ran away, I was a senior in high school. Fortunately I had enough credits by the end of my junior year to graduate, and only needed to complete a few more scholastic requirements to get my diploma. Through the good graces of my Catholic high school, I was allowed to make up those requirements and, after summer school, graduated in August of 1970. Although I would have blithely walked away from high school without a backward glance, the focused attention of my teachers and my principal prevented me from making that costly mistake.

Reality Sets In—My 20s

What I lacked in knowledge, confidence, and skill, I made up for with enthusiasm and daring. Unfortunately, it didn't take long for reality to set in—I soon discovered that enthusiasm and daring require a solid foundation of distinctions, structures, and strategies that I just didn't have.

It took me a little while to develop the survival instincts to identify opportunities to get ahead in my life. Those instincts kept me on the move. Long before I considered success as an option, my instincts helped me survive through seeking out those experiences that would best help me grow.

My search took me through a series of dead-end jobs in Poughkeepsie. After leaving the drug store, I worked in a variety of retail stores where I soon grew bored and restless. Then I got the opportunity to get into the Neighborhood Youth Corps program, where I moved through a number of positions that left me bored and restless again and ultimately got me thrown out of the program for being "willful and unsalvageable."

I lasted ten months at my job as a telephone operator for New York Telephone Company in 1972. That was back when you used to have to dial "0" to make all but local calls. Although I got numerous commendations for helping people place difficult calls to faraway places, I had difficulty following the rules of "six calls a minute— not six minutes a call." It was a mutual parting of the ways when it was clear that I had my own way of interacting with our customers and I wasn't going to change.

After I ran out of all the other options for work in Poughkeepsie, I even waitressed at a Howard Johnson's and a local pancake house. I was terrible at it. My dear friend Barbara, who worked with me at HoJo's and was spectacular at her job, told me later, "I knew you were going to amount to something in life because you sucked as a waitress!"

My personal life wasn't much better. I broke up with my lovely boyfriend in the summer of 1970 because I knew I was not cut out to settle in Poughkeepsie, marry before I was twenty, and start birthing a family of kids. After that I seemed to find every guy in the area who was bad news for me. Heartbreak was a regular occurrence; date rape on several occasions in the next ten years was the price of my ignorance and my hunger for someone to love my wounded heart.

Maia, the Sailor

My big break came when I enlisted in the US Navy just before I turned twenty-one. My father had to sign my enlistment form even though I was an emancipated minor in New York State. My intention was to get as far away from Poughkeepsie as I could; my father told me as he signed the paperwork that he thought that was a very good idea.

During my eleven and a half years in the Navy, I got the greatest education of my life. One of the first things I learned was that I would rather sandblast and paint submarines on a floating dry dock than work as a secretary or in the personnel office—traditional jobs for females.

When the Navy started putting women on ships in 1975, I was the third woman to report for duty on the USS San Onofre (ARD-30) where I stayed for three years. I was the first woman to make rate; that is, to earn non-commissioned officer (NCO) status as a third class petty officer. I learned how to drive a two-ton pickup truck with a standard transmission so I could travel all over San Diego as the ship's supply petty officer. I made friends with the suppliers of the marine equipment we needed for dockings and un-dockings. I was the only woman in my class when I attended both Basic and Advanced Firefighting and Damage Control Schools. And I learned how to supervise the young men who were junior to me—guys who were younger than me, taller than me, and had been in the Navy longer than me, who clearly hadn't been raised by their mamas to take orders from "no girl." The Navy was teaching me leadership skills with real-world applications!

Although I was learning leadership skills from my two exceptional supervisors on the San Onofre, I was very green at it. In a Navy in which women were just starting to develop their power as leaders, I was very rough around the edges. My goal was always to develop my leadership abilities so my supervisors would be proud of me; along the way I alienated some of the other (male) supervisors and many of the crew. Once again, I had to learn things my own way. Ultimately, I didn't make a lot of friends. On several occasions, when my supervisors were on vacation or not around to protect me from my own ignorance, I got into trouble by providing those who wanted to knock me down to size the opportunity to use Navy regulations to show me who was really in charge. Once again, I felt angry and isolated.

Out of the Navy—Into the Frying Pan

After my three years on the *San Onofre*, I was ready to get out of the Navy. I was twenty-five years old. Six months earlier, I had begun working with a therapist, Gwen Nichols. I found her at San Diego County Mental Health when I realized that I was down to two alternatives in my life: suicide or therapy. I knew I had to be very careful which one I chose first—and I got lucky. Gwen parented me in ways I had never been parented and showed me what I was made of by engaging me in my own recovery. She absolutely changed my life. She set me on the path to healing, even though it took several more years for me to walk it in a conscious way.

Over the next two years, I wired small boats in the shipyards, installed residential solar heating units, and, based on my knowledge of air conditioning and refrigeration, was the first woman hired in the engineering department of the Islandia Hyatt in Pacific Beach. Instead of the exciting HVAC work I thought I'd be doing, I found myself caulking bathtubs, unplugging toilets, and changing light bulbs; I only lasted two weeks. Then I moved to Seattle and worked for Pacific Bell, where I didn't last ninety days as a directory assistance operator. Finally I landed a job as the supervisor of the women's locker room at the Bellevue Athletic Club, folding towels and refilling shampoo, conditioner, and body-wash dispensers.

Although most of my work at that time wasn't challenging or rewarding, there was one significant opportunity for growth and development. At my solar heating job, I was apprenticed to Bob Towers, the crew boss of the installers. Bob knew everything there is to know about installing solar heating units. He was a subcontractor who worked for the company owners who had hired me. We were introduced on my second day on the job. Bob's first words to me—spoken while looking at the ground—were that he "wouldn't work with a girl." (This was in 1978.) I just stood there and looked at him. Then, after a few moments, he looked me right in the eyes and told me he would call me "Boy." I looked right back at him and said I was fine with that. Once we had our relationship established, he treated me like his son—a son he grew to be proud of. He was an excellent teacher, from whom I learned more than I can ever say. I can still hear him saying, "Now, Boy, this is how you want to [do whatever it was]." He only had to show me once, because he let me do it myself after he showed me how. He taught me in my own learning style; I worked as hard as I did for him because I loved him.

After I'd apprenticed with Bob for about six months and had learned everything he could teach me, the owners of the company hired a friend of theirs and made me teach him everything I'd learned. After about a month, they gave that man his own truck and made him my supervisor. That's when I quit.

Maia, the Sailor—Again

Six months after that, I was sitting in the Bellevue Athletic Club one boring afternoon when it suddenly dawned on me that my only chance at financial security was to go back to the Navy and "do it right this time." At that point, I'd completely given up on love and happiness—I'd decided I didn't need them. This was a practical decision. I also knew that I didn't want to be an unmarried enlisted woman, prey to the kind of relationship problems with sailors that I'd had before. I married a man I didn't love so I could get back to work, get on with life, and not be an old maid. Now twenty-seven years old, I was clearly past my prime; women my age were married and had kids. It was obvious that no one was ever going to love me like my first boyfriend had, and frankly I didn't care. I knew I'd be a divorcee in a very short time, and that was fine with me.

Armed with all the intelligence of a Navy background and the connection to my dear friend George (my former warrant officer from the *San Onofre* who had become a surrogate dad to me), I went back into the Navy with training for a new job assured and my plan laid out. I was one of only a few women in Basic Electricity and Electronics School, followed by Interior Communications School, where I learned to operate and repair all of the communication gear on a ship. Bob Towers had trained me well; I graduated third in my class.

According to my plan, things should have worked out smoothly — if dully — from there on out. Nothing could have been further from the truth.

In less than a year, my marriage crashed and burned in a big way and I found myself in love with a sailor from my ship. By 1980, the Navy was sending women out to sea. The first ship that headed out from Norfolk with women on board was mine, the *USS Vulcan (AR 5)*. It was a very heady time for me: a shipboard romance out at sea, the power to choose what my heart wanted, and the knowledge that maybe there was going to be happiness for me after all.

After finding happiness in love after all this time, I was still very conflicted about my need to free myself from a man I never should have married in the first place. In the midst of my happiness, I saw his despair as all my fault — even though his behavior completely warranted my departure. In the midst of this situation, I was transported back to the circumstances of my childhood, when everything that went wrong was my fault.

Although I didn't know it at the time, now I'm clear that every obstacle brings a gift. My impending divorce quickly brought me its gift. In my distress over my husband's situation, I reached out for help again and was plugged in to the Navy's substance abuse recovery community. I received a thirty-day outpatient treatment as a "co-dependent," and learned about dysfunctional family systems and the beliefs we accept as children that negatively impact our lives long after we leave home.

A co-dependent was described to me as "someone who, on their deathbed, sees someone else's life flash before their eyes." This is someone who is so enmeshed in another person's life that they have no power over their own. That was me. Eleven years after I'd left my home, I was still a little girl who thought her mother's illness and her father's rage were *all her fault*. The gift my first husband gave me was being the catalyst for me to find the resources to heal this wound.

Over the next three years, I took every training the Navy had for substance abuse recovery. Within four years, I became a certified counselor myself, first in the Navy and then as a civilian.

Within two years, during the week of my thirtieth birthday, it suddenly dawned on me that there had to be a purpose for my life. That realization stopped me in my tracks. It gave me the reason to start paying attention in ways I never had before.

Fortunately, I was working in the field of substance abuse counseling. In the course of my work, I was learning a lot about my family dynamics and the effects that generations of alcoholism, on both sides of my family tree, had had on my parents—and on our family. Most important, I was discovering distinctions about things that I had previously thought were only true about me.

I was astonished to learn that other people felt as negatively about themselves as I did about myself; that they felt as lonely, frightened, and ignorant as I did. More astonishing than that, I learned that there are people in this world whose mission it is to take others through the process of recovery that they have traveled themselves. That's when I realized that I had found my work in the world.

A New Beginning

In 1987, I was honorably discharged from the Navy as a petty officer first class (E-6). I was years into my own recovery work and was helping others find recovery as well. I had married the sailor I'd fallen in love with in Norfolk. Being a part of his family and loving him the best I could taught me more than I could have learned anywhere else about what I needed to do to create a thriving relationship and love someone with my whole heart. Although my life was improving significantly on multiple levels, everything I was learning shed a glaring light on all the unresolved difficulties in this relationship. Despite our best attempts, our marriage did not survive my recovery.

Although it took me almost twenty years of trials and errors, dead ends, and turnarounds, I finally realized that much of what I ran away from home to escape had traveled with me. More important, in my recovery work I also came to realize that a substantial amount of what I brought with me gave me courage and stamina I wouldn't otherwise have had.

In the process of my recovery, I finally realized that everything I'd been through had a purpose—if only I would harness it. Out of the Navy just thirty days and working as a counselor at Charter Hospital, I created a program called Stress Arresters. In it I shared my strategies for creating a thriving life with clients and audiences in Corpus Christi for more than two years.

Twenty years after I ran away from home, another day changed my life. On December 19th, 1989, I met Chuck Beatty. Several weeks earlier, he had called me at my office to hire me to present *Stress Arresters* to his workgroup, and, as I found out shortly thereafter, had fallen in love with me over the phone.

In less than three weeks, we began a relationship that has been a constant source of joy, learning, and fulfillment for over twenty-two years. In the first week of our relationship, Chuck said, "I think you should do your dream and you should let me help you."

The work I've done that has become the *Journey to Powerful Presence* is my dream—and Chuck has worked by my side every step of the way to make it come true.

Dance into Your Power

Chapter 3

You Can Only Guide Someone Where You've Been Before

Although my meeting with Chuck changed my life in ways that directly led me to discover my own Powerful Presence, I was only ready for him because I had spent all those years after my initial treatment for co-dependency working my recovery, learning additional lessons, and translating what I learned for other people.

It took me a while to clear my head of all the negativity I'd brought with me. Until I looked back on it, I had no idea what I was learning along the way. In the process of becoming the person I now knew I wanted to be, and creating the work I now believed I was on the planet to do, three experiences grounded me solidly on my path to Powerful Presence:

1. Years of therapy with several gifted therapists who helped me unravel the mysteries of my feelings and the structures

of my beliefs about myself. Many of the strategies I learned from them or created while I was working with them found their way into the Journey to Powerful Presence.

2. My training in the Navy as a substance abuse counselor, which allowed me to make new distinctions and uncover new structures and strategies for creating a happy and successful life. During the eight years I worked in the field, as both a certified Navy counselor in California, Florida, and Texas and a civilian counselor certified in the State of Texas, I created programs and presentations that allowed me to share what I learned with other people. Their successes with my strategies fueled a passion in me that birthed my careers as a keynote speaker in 1987, a communication strategist and trainer in 1990, a published author in 1995, and a co-active coach in 2004.

3. My training in Neurolinguistic Programming (NLP), which I began as a Navy substance abuse counselor in 1984, transformed my perception of my experience. With NLP I discovered the structures we use to create our experience and the strategies available to us to shift it in the blink of an eye. NLP helped me create even more powerful strategies for myself; using it allowed me to get more conscious of my own actions than anything I've learned before or since. NLP is at the heart of the Journey I've created to Powerful Presence and all the work I do as a speaker, trainer, and coach.

By the time I'd put together everything I'd created in my career and discovered that there was a Journey to Powerful Presence—and I knew how to take it—another twenty years had passed.

It was the spring of 2009. I'd been in business for myself for almost twenty years, and, like lots of other business owners, I'd had periods of great success as well as periods of great disappointment. Chuck and I had moved several times to different parts of the country, chasing business opportunities and the quality of life that was important to us. Each time we moved, there was a period of readjustment, of building up my business again.

Our last move was to Northeast Ohio, where we arrived just in time for the economy to crash. One spring morning, I was sitting in our living room trying to make sense of my life. It dawned on me that I was almost fifty-seven years old and it had been almost forty years since I'd started creating my life. Once again, I seemed to be at a stalling point with my business. In a way I hadn't done in years, I spent the morning doubting myself with one question: "What is the point of everything I've done?"

After all those non-traditional jobs and my training as a certified substance abuse counselor, I'd been a successful international keynote speaker and trainer, and traveled all over the US, Canada, the UK, Australia and the Dominican Republic. I'd inspired millions of people. I had a PBS video and three books to my name. I'd trained and coached lawyers in Australia in two separate week-long negotiation classes as the only woman on the training team— and the only woman in the room. I'd trained seasoned trainers at the Occupational Safety and Health Administration (OSHA) and in multinational corporations like Make-up Art Cosmetics (MAC) and Research in Motion (the makers of the Blackberry). I'd coached many amazing clients who'd all gotten remarkable results from our work together.

That morning, as I wrestled with my doubts, none of it mattered.

My suffering was the result of the fact that I simply couldn't see where to go or what to do next. It was worse than the feeling of ignorance I'd had in my twenties, because I was sure that I really ought to know better.

That morning, I'd forgotten one truly important and amazing thing about my life: Once I'd left home, no one ever told me what to do.

This is different from taking orders in the Navy, or doing what you're told to do on a job. In everything I did with my life, I made up what to do by myself. If it made sense to me, I'd do it, no matter what anyone else said or did. I've made my most memorable mistakes that way, as well as created my most significant successes.

My secret was this: Every step of the way, I'd act like I knew what I was doing even when I didn't. What brought me so much success was my willingness to step up to the proverbial plate and take action. Just like I learned all those years ago in my first NLP training: Action is the trademark of knowledge.

As soon as I remembered that, I got into action. After spending the morning wrestling with my feelings of ignorance, I realized I needed to spend the rest of the day creating a map for myself.

Whenever I get stuck in an overwhelming emotion, I have to transform my feelings into something visual. In the process, I've learned that this is my most successful strategy for finding my way through anything, including the most difficult circumstances. For the rest of that day and into the next two, I mapped out everything I knew—with scented colored markers on Post-it® note sheets of flip-chart paper—and tried to make sense of it all.

By the end of those three days, I discovered the pattern in everything I'd done: my keynotes, my training sessions, my coaching, and my books. Every single thing I'd done had helped other people identify, access, and claim their personal power. And everything I'd taught them came from the Journey I'd taken over the last forty years to identify, access, and claim my own. I could see that there were Three Empowering Beliefs, Three Resourceful Abilities, and Three Focused Actions that had been at the heart of all of it.

The biggest gift of the whole process was realizing that if I hadn't suffered that overwhelming doubt in myself, I'd never have discovered the treasure trove that was waiting for me: the map of the Journey to Powerful Presence and those three beliefs, three abilities and three actions it requires.

As I began to share what I had learned with others, I realized there's a pattern to the Journey that we all must travel. Although our circumstances are unique, the pattern is the same. That's what makes the process I discovered so useful.

In the next chapter, you'll find my map of the Journey to Powerful Presence. You'll get a look at where we're headed and see how each stage of the Journey provides you with the foundation for what follows.

Dance into Your Power

Part Two

Prepare for the Journey

Dance into Your Power

Chapter 4

Mapping the Journey

Spending those three days in my living room and kitchen helped me see at a distance those things that were invisible to me when I was living through them. With a detached perspective and a curious mind, those patterns of distinctions, structures, and strategies that I'd built revealed themselves to me. It was clear that I'd been on a forty-year Journey, and that every single part of it positioned me to get to the next stage of my life.

I discovered that I had built my success on Three Empowering Beliefs, Three Resourceful Abilities, and Three Focused Actions. They weren't obvious when I was building on them—they required hindsight to appear.

Three Empowering Beliefs

After those three days, I could see that many things I believed about myself in the early parts of my Journey held me back and kept me down. They filtered my experience in ways that kept me traveling in circles, over and over again, returning to the same kind of situations that reinforced my negative beliefs about myself. I would end up feeling even more worthless as a human being, more dejected about my circumstances, and more clueless about how I kept landing there.

In my mid-twenties, I finally found Gwen Nichols, the great therapist I mentioned in Chapter 2, who got me started on the path that led me to create the Journey to Powerful Presence. She helped me take my first look at those negative beliefs and the myriad ways they had me bound in chains. She opened the door to this book; she gave me the foundation from which to begin it.

By the time I hit my thirties, I had put enough of what I learned from her into practice that I was ready for the next stage in learning about my beliefs.

As a substance abuse counselor in the 1980s, I learned about the effect of affirmations on my beliefs about myself from Rokelle Lerner, who wrote the book called *Affirmations for Adult Children of Alcoholics*. During my time as a Navy counselor, I had a clinical supervisor who worked diligently to help me get conscious of how badly I beat myself up when I made a mistake or failed to be less than stellar in every given moment. He helped me overcome the disparity between the powerful work I was doing with others and the disempowering way I was treating myself by showing me how to use daily, focused affirmations to reset my inner conversation. He showed me how to use these affirmations to overcome the damage that my negative beliefs about myself were having on my life. It worked.

A few years later, I was deeply influenced by Louise L. Hay when I read her book *You Can Heal Your Life*. By following her instructions— especially by speaking aloud the affirmation at the end of the book for the recommended three times a day, every day, for about two years—I began to clear the self-limiting fog that my beliefs had created within me. That's when I started trying on other beliefs that I'd learned from Rokelle, Louise, my clinical supervisor Dan Adams, his wife Mary Lou Holt (who was my therapist at the time), and others—beliefs that were more positive and empowering.

My most empowering result was that I changed the way I talked to myself. In the process, I traded in my old beliefs about who I was and what I could do and developed new ones. In the beginning, these new beliefs left me feeling more hopeful; ultimately, they helped me find and create lasting happiness for myself.

When I boiled down everything I'd learned into the three most powerful beliefs I'd developed, I realized that I'd found the ones that fueled my Powerful Presence:

1. You bring about what you think about.
2. You have what it takes.
3. Every obstacle brings a gift.

I was clear that each belief provided the foundation for the one that followed.

You Bring About What You Think About

Although identifying and choosing this belief took me more than twenty years, once I chose to believe it, my life changed immediately. The minute I connected my results to the beliefs I held about myself, I changed the way I chose my thoughts. Once I realized that I could either suffer over my circumstances or reframe them as the set-up for developing my character and learning new skills, I was hooked on choosing my thoughts wisely. In 1995, I wrote my first book, *Bootstrap Words: Pull Yourself Up!*, about the power of this belief. The Journey to Powerful Presence is only possible because of it.

You Have What It Takes

Identifying this one took me another ten years. Even though I'd worked through a tremendous amount of self-doubt with two great therapists in my twenties and thirties, I still held on to the belief that I could only do so much before I failed. Then one of my teachers reminded me of something I'd heard years before: "We're all making stuff up all the time that is only true for us because we say so. Why don't you make up something that will serve you instead of defeat you?"

Once I chose this belief, I never looked back. Believing it actually shifted my physical experience when tackling something important and difficult. Now, instead of that rush of anxiety I used to feel as I imagined that others would soon see that I was making everything up and had no clue what I was doing, I feel relaxed and expectant. We're *all* making things up! Now I'm making up things that help me embrace difficulties as well as success. This belief is the key.

Every Obstacle Brings a Gift

In hindsight, this one is easy to believe. Whenever I think of the obstacles I've overcome in the past tense, it takes little effort to see that I've learned new skills and developed beneficial qualities as a result of those experiences. That's something we all have in common. Obstacles are meant to be our teachers. Struggling through and making mistakes is how humans learn. This belief takes that fact to the next level.

Hindsight gives you the understanding of your learning and growth after the fact; taking it to the next level means that you believe in your learning and your growth in the midst of the obstacle instead of afterward. When you focus on the gift of every obstacle, you reduce your suffering immeasurably. When you reduce your suffering, your brain works better and you're exponentially more resourceful.

When you believe that you bring about what you think about, you can easily shift your focus from the obstacle to the gift. When you believe that you have what it takes, you're confident that this obstacle will have something to teach you.

By the time I finished identifying these three beliefs, I was clear that they form the foundation of Powerful Presence and prepare you for the next stage of your Journey.

Three Resourceful Abilities

Now that I had identified the Three Empowering Beliefs, I had a feeling that there was another element involved in mapping out the Journey to Powerful Presence.

Since my teachers and role models were very skilled in distinctive ways, I identified their abilities in terms of Powerful Presence. As I did so, it became very clear that although they possessed a wide range of specialties and personality styles, they had these three abilities in common:

1. Walk your talk with integrity.
2. Relate to others.
3. Dance with whatever shows up.

Once I identified these abilities, I realized they were the foundation of all of my successes. Although I was unaware of their synchronicity as I was learning them and using them on my own Journey, once I surveyed everything I'd created over the last twenty years in my keynotes, trainings, and books, each one stood out like a beacon.

Walk Your Talk with Integrity

For my teachers, *walk your talk with integrity* meant they knew who they were and what they stood for—they were comfortable in their own skin. They knew what they knew. Although they were adept at sharing it, they didn't feel a need to prove it. Being authentically themselves was the truth of their being. Whether you agreed with them or not was completely up to you.

Ram Das pointed the way to my understanding of this in 1971 when I found a copy of his book *Be Here Now* in a bookstore in New

York City. Although I didn't fully appreciate it for another thirty-five years, I was astounded by what he was pointing to: "You're enough! Just be present in the moment, wherever you are. Wake up—there's nothing to prove."

Gwen Nichols, my first therapist, pointed me in this direction as she worked to introduce me to myself. She started me on the road to being conscious of the possibility that I was perfect just the way I was, at a time when all I could see was the enormity of my imperfection.

When you walk your talk with integrity, you're conscious of your actions and your impact. As I was learning how to do this, I discovered there's a process to it:

1. The first thing you have to do is get conscious of what's coming out of your mouth and determine whether it matches your actions. That's the only way you can identify what you're doing and saying.
2. As you're learning to get conscious, you have to keep adjusting your words to match your actions and your actions to match your words. It takes time and patience, yet the more you do it the easier it gets, because you learn to access at will that ability to match your words with your actions.
3. Finally, you have to be willing to put what you know into practice in every circumstance, despite anyone else's opinion of it.

This is a tall order, I know. I have to admit that over the last forty-plus years I've learned as much about the power of walking my talk by failing miserably at it as I have by getting it right. The good news is that once I identified it, I knew this was the primary ability of Powerful Presence. This is the ability upon which the other two are built.

Relate to Others

When you're comfortable in your own skin, it's much easier to relate to others in a powerful way that benefits you and them. When it's totally OK to be yourself, it becomes totally OK to accept that everyone else is simply being themselves, too.

This second ability was easy to identify, since I consciously pursued it to help me overcome the circumstances of my life. The communication breakdowns in my family had shaped my early life; for many years, I was on a mission to figure out how I could become skilled at communicating in ways that would someday help me prevent breakdowns in my future relationships. Once I turned thirty, I sought out teachers and role models who were exceptional at communicating in a variety of contexts, and I learned everything I could from them.

All my teachers and role models were adept at relating to others in a powerful way because of their exceptional communication skills. In the course of my work with them, they taught me that communication breakdowns are simply a part of life. Getting skilled at picking up the pieces when things go wrong is a major component of the work I've been doing for the last twenty years, and I knew this ability was another foundation of Powerful Presence.

My teachers and role models taught me that communication breakdowns provide opportunities for breakthroughs, too—when you're ready and willing to have the kind of conversation that allows both parties to hear each other and be heard by one another.

Breakdowns help you sit up and pay attention; they help you get conscious of the part you contributed to the problem.

Breakthroughs are always the result when you get conscious. Sometimes, both parties have a breakthrough, and their relationship deepens immeasurably. Other times, only one person has a breakthrough, and I've learned that that's OK. Although the current relationship may fail as a result of the unresolved breakdown, the person who remains conscious can use everything she learned in the process to prevent—or work through—that kind of breakdown in a future relationship. Either way, breakdowns are a part of life.

Mastering this ability allows you to exponentially develop your Powerful Presence. As you master its distinctions, structures, and strategies, you can avoid many breakdowns in the first place—simply because you're being pro-active. When you can't avoid a breakdown, those same distinctions, structures, and strategies will help you maneuver through it with the best chance of having a breakthrough. As you continue to develop these first two abilities, you will find that it's so much easier to dance.

Dance with Whatever Shows Up

When you walk your talk with integrity, relating to others is much easier. When you relate to others authentically, you'll find that you already have much of what you need to start dancing.

Before I came up with the words to describe Ability #3, I knew it had to encompass all the ways that someone with Powerful Presence stays flexible despite circumstances, and finds ways to maneuver through whatever shows up with a positive and powerful approach. There's a particular reason why I chose the word dance.

Dance had to be the operative word because it means your whole body is involved. This isn't an intellectual exercise; you're using everything you've got to engage with your circumstances. There's a power in dancing that trumps just about anything else in keeping you flexible and moving—it's the exact opposite of being stuck.

It's only over the last eight years that I've come to believe I'm a dancer. Because of my experiences, I've also come to believe that everyone else is a dancer, too, even though many people just don't know it yet. Many of us were taught that only certain people have the talent to be dancers, and that the rest of us should refrain from trying. I believed that for over fifty years. Then I met a dance teacher in a movie called Mad Hot Ballroom who changed my life.

Pierre Dulaine has changed the world of dance with his global performances since the 1960s. The only reason I had the privilege of discovering him was because he changed the lives of children with his Dancing Classrooms project in New York City.

When I "met" him in the movies about this project—Mad Hot Ballroom and Take the Lead—I was astonished at the simplicity of his message. First, that dance is the medium through which life skills can be taught, and second, that everyone can dance. In the movie Take the Lead, he's played by Antonio Banderas. The line that will never leave me is this one: "Can you walk? If you can walk, you can dance. Look! You're dancing!"

And learning to dance—in my fifties—transformed my presence. In doing so, I learned something that Pierre already knew: Dancing is simply a vehicle for moving through your life. You can plod, you can crawl, you can walk, and you can run if you like. Yet when you dance, you transform the nature of every experience into a kind of joy.

People with Powerful Presence exude that kind of joy. That's what I wanted to share on this Journey, so that's how this ability came to be named.

Three Focused Actions

The process of discovering the elements of Powerful Presence was exhilarating, and I knew there was one more element to discover. It was clear that having those Three Empowering Beliefs was the foundation of the Journey. Developing the Three Resourceful Abilities was the next stage. Then I realized that everything I'd put together so far was irrelevant unless those beliefs and abilities were put into action and practiced on a regular basis.

Once again, I looked at what I had learned and taught; once again, I found a pattern of action:

1. Use what you know.
2. Share what you've learned.
3. Create something new.

Use What You Know

The saying "Use it or lose it" applies as much to Powerful Presence as it does to exercise. Beliefs and abilities become instinct only with practice. As I thought about my history, it was clear that although these beliefs and abilities had taken me time to identify, once I started using them regularly they became instincts.

When I first started my Journey, I was always faced with a choice: to do what I had always done or choose a new way. The more I chose my new beliefs and developed my abilities, the easier it became to choose them. A neuroscientist would tell you that I was creating new neural pathways every time I chose new behavior until I had completely rewired my brain.

Share What You've Learned

A math teacher of mine once told me that the best way to learn something new was to teach it to someone else. This is just as true with math as it was for me on my Journey to Powerful Presence.

Once I started getting results with my new behaviors—choosing the beliefs and developing the abilities of Powerful Presence—I wanted to share what I'd learned with everyone who needed it. This led me to create all of my keynote speeches and training courses, starting in 1987, and to write my first three books, starting in 1995.

The more I taught what I knew, the more it was reinforced in my life. There were many occasions when something I'd just taught in a class, shared in a keynote, or used with a coaching client would be just the thing I needed in some challenging situation. There it was, right in my recent memory, with all the power it had when I'd used it to help someone else. Sharing what I knew was one of the ways I learned to walk my talk with integrity—since I couldn't speak it to others without using it myself.

Create Something New

At the end of my three days of soul-searching, I realized that this third action was the ultimate result of my search. It was also the one practice I'd been doing naturally for forty years. As a result of running away from home, I systematically created a new life for myself. When I was developing my abilities as a substance abuse counselor, it made perfect sense to me to create new ways to express what I'd learned so I could share it with others. All of my keynote speeches, my training classes, and my books were the result of my understanding that in order to make an experience your own, you have to claim it for yourself by creating something new with it. That's what makes it yours and not a copy of someone else's.

If it's true that each of us has a purpose on this planet (and I believe that it is), and that each of us has a gift that the world needs, then this map of the Journey to Powerful Presence is my purpose. It's a composite of everything I've learned over the last forty years in a completely unique way that only I can put into words.

Here's Where You Come In

I love the idea that when the world's need intersects with your talents and gifts, you will find your purpose in life. This work is my purpose. My hope is that by taking the Journey to Powerful Presence yourself, you will find yours.

If you were taking this Journey with me in a live or teleclass version, we would take twelve weeks to cover all the material in this book. You can take the Journey in your own way when you travel with me. There are several ways you can use this book to do that:

1. Read it straight through, so you can get a sense of the Journey before you take it.
2. When you're ready—either the first time or later—read it in small sections, as if you were taking the Journey in real time. Do the exercises and experience the changes that develop in your life.
3. Use it as a resource once you've completed your Journey. Go back and re-read those chapters that draw you back. Take the time to try a practice you haven't tried yet or re-experience a practice you tried months or years before. This Journey awaits you at any point in your life, and it will be different each time you take it.

Should you decide to just start the Journey as you read this book for the first time, let me share with you one of the things I learned as a substance abuse counselor: It takes every bit of ninety days to begin to change your life. This book contains everything you need to get started; the ingredient you add is time.

Take your time on this Journey.

The Dancers in my classes tell me that although twelve weeks seems like a long time at the beginning, the time flies by faster than they imagined. My guess is that the time flies because each of them is in action for her life. That makes all the difference.

Now that you know where we're headed, let's take the next step together. In the next section, there are a few things you'll need to do to get ready to take this Journey. Just like any trip you'd take anywhere, you need to plan and pack!

Chapter 5

Getting Ready to Travel

Now that you know about Powerful Presence and you've seen where it began, I hope you're ready to start your own Journey. The rest of this book contains the distinctions, structures, and strategies that allow you to become a more authentic you, so you can dance into your power and create remarkable results anywhere you want them in your life.

This is where things get personal.

You're about to embark on a Journey that's all about you: what you want, where you're headed, and what you're willing to do to get there. Think about how you would prepare for the journey of a lifetime. Would you simply wait for your departure date and head out without any planning or preparation? Definitely not.

Getting ready to take a journey is
every bit as important as taking it.

In order to have the most exceptional experience on your trip, you have to get ready. Over the years, I've discovered three basic strategies that will get you ready to travel anywhere:

- Decide how you want to capture your experience—in photos, on video, in a journal, or some combination of the three.
- Plan your itinerary so you can do what you want to in the time you have available.
- Pack your bags—make sure you have everything you need for the trip.

In this chapter, you have the opportunity to do those same three things to get ready for your Journey:

Step 1. Determine how you'll capture your experience.
Step 2. Create your itinerary.
Step 3. Pack your mental "bags" with one essential accessory.

Step 1: Determine How You'll Capture Your Experience

Did your family take home movies when you were growing up? Do you have digital or hardcover photo albums? Have you ever kept a journal?

If you answered yes to any of those questions, you know how powerful it is to revisit the memorable experiences you've had in the past. It feels good to take the trip all over again—maybe share it with friends. More often than not, you're surprised by things that were invisible to you when you were in the midst of the experience.

To get the most out of this Journey, the first thing you need to do is plan to capture your experience by creating a travel journal. Keeping this journal will allow you to personalize your Journey in your own unique ways—ways that will direct you to opportunities you can't even imagine here at the beginning.

No matter what form your journal takes, keeping a record of your experiences will give you more insights on how to develop your Powerful Presence than anything I can tell you in this book. It's your personal experience that will show you exactly what route to take on your Journey.

Make it a point to create your journal now so you can capture everything else that follows. You can make it as high-tech as a document on your computer or as simple as a school notebook from an office supply store. It's your Journey and your journal; whether you keep it streamlined and functional or get wildly creative is completely up to you.

I created a PDF of a journal template for you that contains all of the action items in this book. You can find it at *www.maiabeatty.com/PDFs/myjournal.pdf*. You can print it out and follow along with the book as you record your experiences, thoughts, and answers in it.

> **Take Action**
>
> Create, download, or buy your journal.

Step 2: Create Your Itinerary

Now that you've got your journal, you're ready for the next part of your preparation. This involves two ingredients: first you set your intentions, and then you create an itinerary that will best suit those intentions.

Ingredient One: Set Your Intentions

What are intentions, anyway? Are they really just those bricks you've heard about, with which the road to hell is paved?

Intentions are the internal guideposts of your desires.

They're the indicators of whether or not you're traveling where you want to go, achieving what you want to achieve and behaving the way you want to behave. You set them. They make sense to you. They're as unique as you are.

What are your intentions for this Journey?

Think about it for a moment with these three questions in mind:

1. Why are you reading this book?
2. What do you want to achieve that you haven't achieved already?
3. What's missing from your presence right now that would really make a difference in your life?

If this is the first time you've thought about these three questions, you may not have any idea where to start. That's not a problem. If you need a good place to start:

- Go back to page 5, and reread the list of seven magnetic behaviors of Powerful Presence. Which one of them would really make a difference in your life if you mastered it?
- Think about the reasons you chose this book. What made you choose it? What did you want to accomplish as a result of reading it?
- Consider the ways you think Powerful Presence will help you achieve what you want, personally or professionally or both. Which is most important to you now?

┌─ **Take Action** ─────────────────────

Take some time alone in a quiet place where you'll be undisturbed and consider your intentions for this Journey. Capture them in your journal.

Ingredient Two: Create Your Itinerary

Now that you know where you're headed, you can create an itinerary for yourself that will help you get there no matter what route you take or what side trips you decide to enjoy. Although you can't plan for everything that will happen along the way, you can definitely claim where you want to go. Your itinerary includes these five elements:

1. **Identify your destination. What do you want to accomplish?**
   Make sure you know where you're headed so you'll know when you're getting closer—or if you're getting off track.
2. **Determine the benefits of arriving at your destination.**
   What's in it for you to take this Journey? How specifically will you benefit as a result?
3. **Identify your strengths as well as your challenges.**
   Both will affect you on this Journey.
4. **Create a graphic description of your success.**
   Start with the end in mind. If you were taking a trip to Hawaii, you'd have a mental picture of where you're going. Any delays or challenges in the travel are completely surmountable when you know where you're headed!
5. **Identify the routes you want to avoid in the process.**
   There's a very important reason to create an itinerary when you travel: it's a map of where you want to go. Anything not included on your itinerary is typically not a part of your trip. On this Journey we take that idea one step further and make note of those places you don't want to go. Should you find yourself getting close to them, you can simply shift your course.

Starting on the next page, you'll find the itinerary I use with my clients. Give yourself the time to answer the itinerary questions in your journal, in a quiet place where you won't be disturbed.

You may find it even more illuminating to have someone you trust ask you the questions and record your answers for you. This dialogue can help you uncover thoughts and ideas that don't immediately come to mind when you're by yourself. Dialogue with a trusted friend or a coach helps you dig deeper than you can by yourself.

F of the template I use with my clients, go to *www.
.com/PDFs/myitinerary.pdf.* You can print these pages out
our friend, or your coach can record your answers on the
template.

Your Itinerary

Element One: Identify Your Destination

Where in your life do you want to have more Powerful Presence?

(Yes, you may have already answered this question in your journal. Consider that answer as your first pass at it. Asking this question again will help you refine your answer. When I use this itinerary with my clients, we find that we only get to the heart of what they want when we ask this question several times. Each time you ask it, you uncover a more profound level of answer—we call this "digging deeper." Allow yourself to dig deeper than the first answer you come up with—this is one place where repetition creates clarity.)

Element Two: Determine Your Benefits

A. *What will accomplishing [your answer to Element One] do for you? How will accomplishing it benefit you?*
   (Think about the payoff you'll get for accomplishing what you've identified in Element One. Your answer to this question will identify your motivation to do what you need to do to get what you want. Before you start out on your Journey, it's very useful to know what really matters to you. When the going gets tough, the benefits you identify here will help you keep moving through the inevitable challenges you will encounter.)

B. *What will accomplishing [your answer to A above] do for you?*
   (This is a very different question—even though it looks exactly the same. It takes you more deeply into the benefit you just identified so you're investigating what's underneath it. This is another opportunity to dig deeper. This question helps you identify the desire that fuels the benefit you've identified. Your answer is your greatest motivator, since it's currently a deep desire of yours that's not satisfied.)

Element Three: Identify Your Strengths and Challenges

A. *Strengths: Consider your answer to Element One. Where do you already do this well, in any context in your life?*
(This is how you identify your strengths—your hidden reserves that will help you face the challenges of your Journey. Many people are surprised that identifying their strengths is such a powerful strategy. Your strengths are your resources, and you can only use the resources that you're aware you have. If you've ever done anything that even remotely resembles what you want to accomplish in Element One, in any context, at any point in your life, be sure to identify it here. If you can't think of any of your strengths, ask someone who knows you well, or work with a coach you trust.)

B. *Challenges: Consider your answer to Element One. What stops you from doing this right now? What challenges do you face?*
(This is how you identify all the things that are currently standing in your way. They are also the reasons why you haven't been able to accomplish what you want to accomplish—yet. These are the obstacles to your progress that this Journey will help you overcome. Being aware of them is your first step in overcoming them.)

Element Four: Create a Graphic Description of Your Success

If you had Unlimited Cosmic Power, money was no object, and you knew you could not fail, what would be true for you when you accomplish your answer to Element One?

(This is the closest representation you can evoke right now of the life you're creating by taking this Journey. This is starting with the end in mind. Once you graphically describe your success, you'll be able to immediately tell which behaviors bring you closer to your destination and which behaviors take you farther away. This distinction prepares you to bring about what you think about.)

Element Five: Identify the Routes You Want to Avoid

If you knew that you could accomplish anything you set out to do on this Journey, what would you want to avoid at all costs?

(This is your final preparation point: assessing your personal boundaries. What would you say no to in order to get what you want? This is the price that you will not pay to get where you're going. Some examples of this are: wanting to be a famous speaker, but not at the risk of losing your family due to the travel and commitment involved; wanting to get to the top of your profession, but not at the risk of damaging your health due to the long hours required. Think about the costs and risks you are not willing to take—now, before you head out. It will save you a lot of headaches later.)

Step 3: Pack Your Mental "Bags" with One Essential Accessory

When you travel to a foreign country, or even to a different region in your own country, you'll find that the people there don't necessarily do things the way you do them at home. Knowing that this is the case, you may find it helpful to bring along some items that will assist you when you encounter customs and ideas that are new and different—even disconcerting.

There is one essential accessory you'll need to travel successfully on the Journey to Powerful Presence: the ability to shift your perspective.

This accessory will benefit you in three ways. It will allow you to:

1. Choose your perspective.
2. Be conscious of how you listen.
3. Choose to listen with empathy.

You'll have ample opportunities to use this accessory on your Journey. In case it's new to you, we're going to take the next chapter to explore it in detail.

Chapter 6

Your Essential Travel Accessory

When you're traveling somewhere that's new to you, it's important to be able to shift your perspective along the way. That's the only way you can see all there is to see, experience every situation as deeply as possible, and understand everything you can from people who speak a different language. This capacity to shift your perspective increases your ability to enjoy the richness of any travel experience—that's what makes it your essential travel accessory.

The purpose of perspective is to allow you to translate what's happening so it has meaning for you.

When you have more than one perspective available to you, you increase your ability to translate what's happening in powerful and positive ways. Being able to access multiple perspectives allows you to:

1. Include the perspective of your own subjective experience.
2. Take into account the perspective of the experiences of others, especially when they're different from yours.
3. Consider every experience with a detached perspective in a logical, objective way.

You have to be willing to shift from one perspective to another if you want to get the broadest possible experience from any situation. This is one of the first distinctions I learned in my NLP training, which labels these different perspectives "perceptual positions." That was certainly a mouthful for me at the time.

Shifting my perspective made more sense to me when I compared it to shifting the gears of my car, since I drove a car with a manual transmission at the time. Shifting gears was something I did as I drove every day. The idea that shifting my perspective could be as simple as shifting the gears of my car helped me tremendously. Several years later, when I was teaching this concept to my clients, the metaphor of shifting gears made it easy.

Have you ever driven a car with a manual transmission? Once you learn how to do it, you find out just how powerful driving can be. You can handle any driving situation simply by shifting the car into the right gear. Although it takes a little while to get used to it, once you get the hang of shifting the gears you can drive anything. The more you practice shifting gears as you drive, the more you discover new ways to handle driving situations, simply because you know how to manually engage every bit of the car's power.

Cars have gears. People have Gears—thinking of it like this will help you to put this metaphor into practice.

If you can imagine that we each have three mental Gears, and that each one represents a particular perspective, you can experience the physical sense of shifting your mental Gears just like you do when you are shifting the gears in your car as you drive. It can be that simple once you get the hang of it.

Using any kind of mechanical gears allows you to move more weight or harness more power than you could by yourself; shifting gears in a car allows you to harness all of the available horsepower in the most effective way.

Now let's extend this metaphor to your brain. Having all three of these mental Gears available to you allows you to engage with anyone, in any circumstance, at a deeper and more powerful level than you could otherwise. When you imagine that each Gear is one perspective, being willing to use all three allows you to simply shift to the specific Gear that will give you the most effective results.

Let's take a look at each of these Gears and explore what how best to engage them.

1st Gear: The Subjective Perspective

- 1st Gear is a reflection of your beliefs, values, opinions, and experiences.
- When you're using 1st Gear, you're *always right*, and what you're experiencing is *always true*—although only for you. It's as if you were your own little planet, so what you're experiencing is always right and true within the boundaries of your subjective self.
- In 1st Gear, you can share what's true for you: your beliefs, your values, your opinions, your experiences. Using 1st Gear allows you to share what you think, feel, believe, and know.

2nd Gear: The Empathetic Perspective

- In 2nd Gear, you can consider someone else's 1st Gear; you can investigate what it's like to live on their planet.
- Using 2nd Gear allows you to imagine what it would be like to walk a mile in someone else's shoes.
- This is the only Gear in which you can listen.

3rd Gear: The Objective Perspective

- In 3rd Gear, you can consider the entire situation using logic.
- Using 3rd Gear allows you to step back and consider the situation from a detached point of view, as if you were an observer. Doing that lets you step away from any emotion you may be feeling so you can see all the facts.
- 3rd Gear is the best one to use when you're making a decision or creating a strategy.

Experience the Gears

It's one thing to identify each of these Gears; what makes them useful to you on your Journey is being willing to use them. Let's take a moment and imagine dancing through each of them so you can claim them for your own.

Dancing in 1st Gear

What do you think about what you just read about the three Gears? Did you agree? Did you disagree? Your response is your 1st Gear— it's the truth for you.

Most of us have no trouble operating from our own 1st Gear. It's our subjective experience; it's the truth for each of us in every waking moment. From this perspective, we know what we know and we're willing to share it; and we know what we want, so we're willing to get out there and get it.

Your 1st Gear is the reason you started this Journey in the first place.

The only challenge with it is that it's an easy place to get stuck. As you travel on your Journey to Powerful Presence, it's important to keep in mind that as true as your 1st Gear is for you, it's only one possibility.

Your 1st Gear is the way you share your beliefs, values, opinions, and experiences with the world. It's a powerful Gear to use when that's what's required. Think of someone you know—from fiction or your life—who acts like their opinions and beliefs are the only ones that matter. That's what it feels like to others when you get stuck in 1st Gear.

The reason this distinction is an essential travel accessory is that you need all three Gears to have the most successful Journey. As you travel through this book with me, you can count on shifting Gears all along the way. Your willingness to shift yourself into and out of 1st Gear when necessary will make all the difference in your experience.

Dancing in 2nd Gear

Have you ever really listened to someone else? When you're successful at it, you've naturally shifted yourself into 2nd Gear. You might not have even been aware of the shift. When you listen well, it's because you understand that the only way to receive anyone's message is to consider what she is saying from *her* perspective.

This is easy to do with someone you love, and relatively easy to do with someone you like or whose opinion matters to you. It's a lot harder to do when you don't know—or don't like—the other person. That's what makes 2nd Gear such a powerful accessory. On your Journey, you will learn how to shift into 2nd Gear any time you like. You will learn how to get curious. You already do this naturally with the people you care about; on your Journey you will learn to use it with anyone, anywhere.

The secret of using 2nd Gear anywhere, with anyone, is to ask yourself this question: "What could be true for this person right now so whatever she's saying or doing makes sense to her?"

The only drawback of 2nd Gear occurs when it's the only one you use. You can hear and see things from someone else's perspective in 2nd Gear; when you don't share your perspective from 1st Gear, no one can discover it.

The secret to your success in using the Gears is to practice shifting in and out of these first two. Use 1st Gear when you're speaking and 2nd Gear when you're listening. Here's why:

When you speak in 1st Gear, you're sharing your perspective with the other person—you're sharing what's true for you. This gives the other person insight into your thoughts, feelings, beliefs, values, opinions, and experiences. This almost always deepens your relationship.

When you listen in 2nd Gear, you're listening from the other person's perspective. You're tapping in to their thoughts, feelings, beliefs, values, opinions, and experiences. This gives you the ability to:

- listen to the actual words
- listen with acceptance of the person and what they're saying
- listen as if the speaker could contribute to you
- listen for what's *not* being said as well as what *is* being said

This is a game-changing skill that only takes your being curious about the other person. Developing this skill is at the heart of Powerful Presence. Without curiosity, you can only listen from 1st Gear. You miss so much of the message! When you're listening from 1st Gear, you can only listen with your own perspective, which prompts:

- judging, so you can analyze what's being said and prepare your argument against it
- invalidating the speaker, because you "know better"
- being ready to interrupt, dispute the message, or look for what's wrong with what is being said
- trying to control the outcome of the conversation

It really is that simple. Your willingness to share what's true for you in 1st Gear and listen to others in 2nd Gear will help you create remarkable results on your Journey. You'll be amazed by what you will be able to see and hear along the way as you do so.

Dancing in 3rd Gear

There are some people who find it very easy to step back and look at things from a detached perspective; they have no trouble shifting into 3rd Gear.

There are some professions that require the ability to shift into 3rd Gear on a regular basis, since an objective perspective is a fundamental aspect of the job. For scientists, medical professionals, engineers, pilots, lawyers, accountants, and financial advisers to consider their data from any other perspective would seem completely illogical to them. And if this sounds a bit like Mr. Spock, that's great. This is the Gear that he was famous for using. If you can imagine Spock as the poster child for 3rd Gear, it will be clear that there are benefits to this Gear as well. This is the Gear you want to be able to access when you need to stay cool under pressure.

Remember Sully Sullenburger, the pilot who landed US Airways Flight 1549 in the Hudson River without a single life lost? He and his crew had to be completely in 3rd Gear to pull that off. No emotion, no hysteria, just a complete understanding of the situation and a single-minded focus on what was required to save the passengers and crew. He made history by staying in 3rd Gear.

The ability to shift into 3rd Gear when you need to will allow you to see the big picture anytime you want to; 3rd Gear is your access to logic without emotion.

Whether using 3rd Gear is new for you or you're already skilled at using it, that's great! You'll have lots of opportunity to use it as you travel. Here's how 3rd Gear works:

1. Step back from the situation and your emotion.
2. Consider the entire situation and all the data at hand, including your behavior.
3. Imagine that you're outside of the situation and can map all of the elements. What can you see and hear from this perspective?

Use the Gear That Fits the Situation

Human beings are hard-wired to feel with emotions and think with logic. We're the only creatures on the planet who have the ability to detach from our emotions and think things through from an objective perspective. We need both our emotion and our logic to be successful in life. We need all three Gears, since none of them are perfect for every situation.

- 1st Gear allows you to identify your beliefs, values, opinions, and experiences and share them with others.
- 2nd Gear allows you to be curious about someone else's 1st Gear so you can walk a mile in their shoes. It's the only Gear in which you can listen.
- 3rd Gear allows you to get a clear idea of what you're facing without getting clouded by emotion. It allows you to see the bigger picture and consider all sides of the issue.

You never know what you're going to run into as you travel through your life. Having three Gears to work with means that you have the greatest amount of choice no matter where you are or what you're doing.

When You Get Stuck and Need Assistance

Although having three Gears gives you the greatest amount of choice, your real-life journey doesn't always happen as neatly as a journey you read about in the pages of a book. In case you get stuck in 1st Gear in a way that isn't working for you, and you can't shift into one that will work better, you may find that you need an alternative.

Here's a strategy that I've found to be very useful when I get stuck: Shift into neutral. I had to invent this alternative to supplement the three Gears when I discovered that I sometimes couldn't shift out of 1st Gear when I needed to.

The idea of shifting into neutral makes a lot of sense when you're driving a car with a stick shift and you're stuck in traffic for a while. Sometimes you can't move forward or back up, and shifting into neutral is the best option until you can decide what to do next.

Shifting into neutral takes the metaphor of the Gears one step further.

When you simply can't shift yourself from some negative emotion in 1st Gear to the detachment of 3rd Gear or the empathy of 2nd Gear, you need a neutral Gear to shift into so you can catch your breath and regroup.

The reason this works is because your emotions are connected to your physiology; when you consciously change your physiology, it affects your emotions in a very positive way.

Let's take a moment to consider the way your emotions affect different parts of your body in 1st Gear. There may be heat or cold; there may be movement, or even a deep stillness. When you start to pay attention to it, you'll find there is a pattern for each of your emotions.

Although we each have a unique way of storing our emotions in 1st Gear, there are general patterns that are the same for most of us. For example, many people store happiness and joy in their chest, in the area of their heart. I find that happiness and joy "hit" me in the chest and then fill me up like those giant helium-filled parade balloons.

Where do you store happiness in your body? This might sound like a very silly question until you carry out some scientific field research and experience it for yourself.

Negative emotions show up in your body, too. Have you ever had a "sinking" feeling in the pit of your stomach? That's an example of experiencing a negative emotion physically that is easy to relate to; that sinking feeling typically indicates dread or fear.

If you ask someone how they experience anger, for instance, many people will tell you that they can feel their anger "rising." Some say their emotions rise from their throat, others say their feet, and others say their chest. When I get angry, it feels like somebody just took a blowtorch to my feet—I'm engulfed in flames in a matter of moments. It took me years to discover that, for me, the strategy of shifting into neutral is the emotional equivalent of dowsing those flames with a cold bucket of water.

Now that you're conscious of the connection between your emotions and your body, it's important to acknowledge that some of us have a stronger emotional connection to our bodies than others. Not everyone on this Journey needs to be able to shift into neutral; it's a practice for those of us whose emotions sweep us away. When you get conscious of how this happens in your body, you can shift into neutral before that emotional tide rises.

If you are one of us, you have to do some pretending. When I discovered this strategy, I needed to find a way to maintain a sense of calm in the midst of some very negative circumstances. It was difficult for me to do until I realized that pretending gets me out of my negative emotion and into a different state of being.

Engaging my imagination is my strategy for getting out of 1st Gear when I've gotten stuck. My feelings run very deep, and I don't take a breath without an emotion. It's still easier than I like to admit for me to occasionally get stuck in anger about something that's hurt me or blindsided me in a negative way. On the occasions when I let my emotions override my sense of peace, engaging my imagination helps me tremendously.

It works like this: When I'm angry or aggravated or in some negative emotional state, I imagine I'm a car engine that's being gunned while sitting in the garage. I can even hear the sound effects, which heighten my sense of what I'm doing to myself. For any car, the best use of those high RPMs is to be purring along out on the open road going somewhere fun—not roaring in the garage!

When I'm very angry, sometimes it takes me a while to see that I'm all revved up and the engine of my emotion isn't working like it should. Eventually, though, the image gets through to me: I'm just stuck in the car in my mental garage, going nowhere, with an out-of-control engine.

Using my car metaphor, it didn't take me long to figure out that I could take it one step further to remedy my out-of-control emotion-engine: shift myself into neutral—just like you would if you were sitting in a real car.

Here's how I do it: I exhale first, loudly. Then I physically take my right foot off the gas (my emotion) and put my left foot on an imaginary clutch. Just shifting my feet like that has an immediate effect on my emotion; these days that one step is usually enough to change my state. Although it might seem very silly to someone whose emotions are less overwhelming, this turns out to be a very powerful strategy for those of us whose negative emotions can run rampant.

There are times when this first step has reduced my negative emotion, yet not completely shifted me out of it. When that happens, I continue to shift myself further into neutral by exhaling several more times slowly (as loudly as I need to), and then saying something like, "Stop. Shift into neutral," in as calm a voice as I can manage, as I jiggle an imaginary stick-shift into neutral with my right hand.

When I use this strategy, I can feel the play in the stick-shift in my imagination—it has a kind of wiggle that lets me know it's really in neutral. Using my right hand to make that motion is a signal to my body that I'm not kidding.

When I successfully shift into neutral, my whole body relaxes, just like you would if you were sitting in a parked car in neutral.

On the few occasions when I need some more movement to work through my emotion, I take it one step further and engage the imaginary emergency brake, just like you would in a real car, to prevent the car from rolling. I make that swift grabbing motion with my right hand and I can hear the noise it makes in my car. At that point, I'm almost laughing, because this really is silly. Silly or not, it works!

After using this strategy for many years, most of the time it doesn't take me long to shift into that neutral state in the midst of an angry one when I:

1. Exhale slowly while I calmly take my right foot off the gas (my emotion) by lifting it up as I push my left foot down on the imaginary clutch. (If you drive an automatic, just put your right foot on the brake pedal and shift the gear stick into neutral.)
2. Say to myself, "Stop. Shift into neutral" a couple of times while I use my right hand to jiggle the stick shift into neutral. (If you drive an automatic, you don't get that jiggle when you shift into neutral. Since using this strategy involves pretending, you have a choice whether to use the jiggle or not!)
3. Make the hand motions of pulling on the emergency brake with my right hand.

What I love the most about this strategy is that it works whether you're standing or sitting, because you're not really driving a car. The secret to its success is the fact that you're using your mind and all of your senses to shift yourself—visualizing yourself shifting into neutral, saying the words to yourself, and using your muscles to move in a way that shifts you into a neutral emotional state.

Why do I keep using this strategy? I have the benefit of remembering how good it feels to circumvent an emotional meltdown simply because I chose to shift my emotions from negative to neutral.

Now you have all three Gears, and a tangible strategy you can use to shift yourself into neutral whenever you need it. From here on out, using the Gears will help you be as resourceful as possible as you travel to the destination you've chosen for yourself.

Before we head out to the next chapter, take a moment to capture what's most important to you about the Gears in your journal—what you write will be what you remember as you're traveling.

Take Action

Journal the top three things you want to remember about the three Gears.

Dance into Your Power

Part Three

Three Empowering Beliefs

Dance into Your Power

Chapter 7

The Journey to Powerful Presence

The Journey to Powerful Presence took me forty years to travel. You're now poised to take it in a fraction of that time. With the help of everything you've read so far, your bags are packed with your most essential travel accessory (the three Gears), you've created your itinerary, and you've started your journal.

Now you're ready to begin your Journey.

During this Journey, you'll be exploring the structure of Powerful Presence and using what you discover to reach your destination. Your travel will include each of the three parts you encountered in Chapter 4 from my map of the Journey:

1. Three Empowering Beliefs
2. Three Resourceful Abilities
3. Three Focused Actions

For each part, we'll explore:

- what it is
- its three elements
- how you can use each one

The rest of your Journey is up to you. Take it at whatever pace feels right to you and record your progress in your journal. Check your itinerary along the way to be sure you're on track.

Have as much fun as possible—and be prepared to be surprised.

Bon voyage!

Chapter 8

A Few Words about Beliefs

It's clear to me at this distance that my beliefs had a powerful impact on my experience. In this chapter, we're going to explore the power of beliefs and the physical reason they have such an impact on our experience.

When you say that you believe something, what are you really saying? Most people will tell you they believe something "because it's true." What's true for you is completely subjective—it's your 1st Gear. Take a moment and consider the things you hold to be true.

We all have beliefs about everything in our lives; when you get conscious about what you believe, you will increase the power of your presence.

> **Take Action**
>
> In your journal, write down ten beliefs you hold—about anything.

In case you're having trouble getting started, here are some examples of beliefs:

- Boys are better than girls are at math and mechanics.
- Girls are excellent at math and mechanics—and anything else they set their minds on.
- Cats are better pets than dogs.
- Dogs are better pets than cats.
- Doing the right thing is easier than you think.
- Driving an American car is a patriotic thing to do.
- Driving a foreign car will keep you safer on the road.
- Flowers are the best way to show someone you love her.
- Having a college degree means you'll get a great job.
- Having children means you won't die alone.
- A hospital is the best place to be when you're sick.
- Staying healthy is the best way to grow old.
- Travel is good for you.
- Volunteering in your community is an important thing to do.
- You shouldn't give handouts to people on the street—they'll just spend it on drugs and alcohol.

Take Action

If you haven't made your own list yet, take a moment now and make one. Feel free to use any items from the list above as a start.

When you look at your list, are the things you've written true for you? Would you say that your actions support your beliefs? For example, if you think travel is good for you, you probably do it as much as you can. If you think travel is bad for you, or unpleasant, you probably do it as little as possible.

Comparing your actions with your beliefs is a great strategy for seeing how congruent they are. It's possible that you'll find some outdated beliefs as well as some very useful ones. Just getting conscious about your beliefs is a great practice. When you're conscious about your beliefs, you'll discover that some of your beliefs are about you, and others are about the world around you.

Your Powerful Presence is made up of your beliefs about *you*. The beliefs you have about everything else have a limited impact on your presence; it's the beliefs you hold about yourself that affect your ability to:

- be conscious of your actions and their impacts
- create spontaneous conversation with anyone, anywhere
- speak, in public or in private, with confidence, flexibility, and ease

So let's take a look at the beliefs you hold about yourself. To help you get started, I've created a list of beliefs that includes those I've held about myself in the past as well as those I currently hold.

Take Action

Use the list below to help you get started, or jump right into your journal and create your own list of the *beliefs you hold about yourself.*

Beliefs about myself that I've held, or still hold, include—and are not limited to—these listed below.

I am:

1. a failure
2. a great dancer
3. a late bloomer
4. despicable
5. disobedient
6. graceful
7. gifted at working with people
8. a skilled traveler
9. perfect, whole, and complete
10. the perfect partner and spouse

11. too big for my britches
12. too sensitive
13. too tall for a girl
14. unlovable
15. very smart

Now that you've made your own list, what do you think about the idea that the beliefs you hold about yourself affect the way you do everything in your life?

One of the reasons this book exists is because I discovered that my beliefs about myself affected everything I did—and didn't do—in my life. When I changed my beliefs, I changed my life. (I wrote about this in 1995 in my first book, *Bootstrap Words: Pull Yourself UP!*)

In this section we're going to explore how your beliefs about yourself affect your life, starting with an exploration of beliefs in general.

Remember the Gears from the last chapter? So far in this discussion, we've explored beliefs from your 1st Gear. That's your subjective experience, which is the truth for you and always right. Your 1st Gear is built with your beliefs, values, opinions, and experiences.

Now we're going to take a look at beliefs from 3rd Gear, with basic behavioral facts that you can check against your experience and explore in ways that will expand your 1st Gear.

What is a Belief?

Our beliefs are the things that we accept as true; this makes them the filters through which we experience the world. If you think of beliefs as the basic building blocks of conscious thought, you will see that:

We use our beliefs to construct our reality.

For example, from my own 1st Gear, when I believed that I was a failure, despicable, and unlovable, my experience of the world was vastly different than it is now. It was as if I was under the spell of some evil sorcerer and, just like in those old fairy tales, nothing good was happening to me. It could have been right under my nose, yet I never saw the opportunity for good since I didn't think I deserved it.

Once I started to change my beliefs about who I was, what I could accomplish, and how I wanted my life to turn out, my experiences began to change. I created work that I'm passionate about, married the love of my life, and moved into the home of my dreams. Looking back, it's very clear to me that my experience of life—and my results in life—have been directly connected to my beliefs about myself.

How about you? If you agree that a belief is simply something that you accept as true, you might also recognize the two other indicators of your beliefs: the way you speak of them and the way you act on them. Do you speak of your beliefs as if they were true? Do you act on them as if they were real?

Where Do Beliefs Come From?

When I decided to map out my beliefs and created the exercise above, I found that my results matched the research, which indicates that beliefs come from three sources:

1. **Accepting the truth from authority.** As we grow up, we're taught what is "true" by the people in our family, school, church, and community. These people are all external sources of authority whose words we accept because of the positions they're in as our parents, teachers, and church or community leaders. As children, we're taught that we don't know enough about the world to decide what's true for ourselves; we need the help of these outside authorities to maneuver our way through the world and understand

the difference between right and wrong. What are some examples of these kinds of beliefs in your early life?

Here are some of mine: good children are quiet, nice girls wear gloves and hats, reading is good for you, parents know everything, *amn't* is a perfectly acceptable contraction, and The Book of the Maccabees is a book in the Bible.

There is no reason to doubt any of these beliefs until you come in contact with something—or someone—who shakes you up with a belief that contradicts it. That takes you to the next source of your beliefs:

2. **Hearing something contrary to your beliefs from another authority or an expert.** As you grow older, you experience more of the world through books, movies, and meeting new people. At some point, you're bound to run into a belief that counters one or more of those your early authorities taught you.

   This happens when you run into one of two contrary sources: another authority who counters what you've been taught with a different "truth," or an expert—someone who has proven through his or her writing, speaking, or teaching that they know what they're talking about.

   The authority has her position behind her; you have to think about what she's said because she's in charge of you. The expert is different. The expert has done the research and come up with results that she has proven to be true in a larger arena and in a scientific way.

   Either way, once you encounter this contrary source, you have to make a decision. You have to choose what you want to believe. That's the action that starts you on the path to becoming the source of your own beliefs. Making those decisions is a part of the job of growing up and learning to make your own way in the world. How did this happen for you?

My experience with contrary authority started early, when I started public school in fourth grade after three years in Catholic school. My teacher, Mrs. Albanese, told me that "the word *amn't* is not a real contraction" when I used it in a sentence. When I argued with her that it was a real word in *my* family, she sent me upstairs to the school library to look it up. My belief in that word was so strong that my failure to find it in the dictionary didn't sway my belief in it for an instant. I went back to class and told my teacher that "just because it's not in the dictionary doesn't mean it's not a real word." I decided to take the word of my family over the word of my new teacher.

My experience with seeking out experts began when I was seventeen and saw on the nightly news that people all over the world were defying the current authority—which was called at the time "the military-industrial complex"—and working to stop the war in Vietnam. Once I saw that it was possible to defy the highest authority on a larger scale than I had ever dreamed possible, I formed the belief that I needed to leave my home. That led me directly to the next source of beliefs:

3. **Generating your own beliefs.** There are three ways you do this:

   a. Trial and error, in which you connect your belief to your experience and decide for yourself what is true for you. Once I ran away from home, I decided what was true for me. Unfortunately, I kept a lot of my old beliefs about myself even though I was deciding on other new beliefs about the way the world worked. It was only when I discovered that some of my beliefs about myself were harming me that I was ready to explore other possibilities.

b. Curiosity, in which you decide to investigate the alternatives for yourself, use all three Gears to explore what you find, and stay open to possibility. This was the work I began when I turned thirty, which I wrote about in Part One.

c. Consciously experiment, in which you pay attention to the results of your beliefs; you modify your beliefs about yourself until you get the results in life that you desire. You consciously connect your experience to those beliefs instead of the other way around. This is the opposite of trial and error. This is the work of the Journey to Powerful Presence.

Take Action

In your journal, map out your experience with beliefs in your own life. Where do your current beliefs come from—external sources, internal sources, or a combination of both?

In the next chapter, we'll explore the physical connection we have with our beliefs.

Chapter 9

Command Central for Your Experience Starts in Your Brain

In the last chapter, we explored beliefs in general—what they are and how we develop them. We also made the distinction that the beliefs that fuel your presence are those you hold about yourself. They make your presence powerful—or not.

In this chapter, we're going to take a walk on the wild side and explore something that is off the beaten path for most of us, unless you happen to be a neuroscientist. We're going to explore the physical connection between your beliefs about yourself and a structure in your brain. We're going to explore the physical reasons why we experience the world the way we believe we will.

First, let's check with your experience. Have you ever walked down an empty street in a neighborhood that's new to you?

- What effect did the time of day have on your experience of your safety? *(What do you believe about being safe in the day versus being safe at night?)*
- How about the kind of neighborhood it was—rich or poor, suburban or city, of your ethnicity or another? *(What do you believe about what you can expect in these different kinds of neighborhoods?)*
- What effect did the country that street was in have on your experience—the US, Europe, Asia, the Middle East, etc.? *(What do you believe about your safety in your own country versus a foreign one?)*

Your answers to the questions above are the result of your beliefs about what's true about an empty street in the circumstances you explored. These beliefs don't reflect what you think about yourself and your abilities; they reflect what you believe about these sorts of circumstances.

Now let's explore some of your beliefs about yourself. Have you ever walked into a large room full of people you didn't know?

- What effect did your beliefs about your skill as a networker have on your experience? *(Did you think you were great at it, or not?)*
- What effect did your beliefs about how well you were dressed have on your experience? *(Did you think your clothes were perfect, or not?)*
- What effect did your beliefs about how smart, knowledgeable, or skilled you are in your profession have on your experience? *(Did you think you had something to offer, or not?)*

Can you see the difference between these two situations? The first one is about your assessment of the environment you're in and what you need to do to remain safe. You decide what you need to do based on your beliefs about those surroundings in those circumstances. You don't need a lot of time to decide; because of your beliefs, your response will be instant. We'll talk about why in a moment.

Now consider the second experience. This one is about your beliefs about *who you are*. The environment isn't changing; the determining factor in your experience is your assessment of *yourself*. Your assessment will either support your Powerful Presence or not. Because of your beliefs, your response will be instant in these circumstances as well. So where does that response come from?

Here's the Scientific Stuff

Current research indicates that in every waking moment we're bombarded with two billion bits of data. We can't possibly process it all, so our brain helps us out.

Deep in our midbrains is a structure that filters the input we receive about the world around us. It's called the *reticular activating system* — RAS for short. The RAS allows us to pay attention to what's happening around us so we can distinguish what's "true" in any given moment.

The RAS filters our experiences through our beliefs; it's almost like a computer program or a particular lens for your camera. For example, looking at the world through rose-colored glasses is the result of a rose-colored filter on your RAS.

The function of the RAS is to filter all of the available data *(two billion bits per second, 24/7!)* so we can make sense of our surroundings and our circumstances.

Can you see how your beliefs about something as simple as your surroundings will have you paying attention to different things depending on what those beliefs are? The same is true about the way your beliefs about yourself filter the way you experience the simple act of walking into a room full of people you've never met. It will either be a wonderful experience that you can't wait to walk into — or the depths of hell you will do anything to avoid! It's only one room, and one group of people, yet two different people will have two completely different experiences. Both experiences happen in 1st Gear, and each is the truth for the individual because of her beliefs.

What makes your beliefs so powerful that they completely determine your experience? The function of the RAS is to ensure our survival. When humans lived in caves, it was critical that they were able to distinguish the factors that would result in *getting lunch* from those that would result in *being lunch*.

When you're walking in an unfamiliar neighborhood late at night, and you're afraid, your RAS is filtering for danger so you don't come to harm. If you believe that you know how to maneuver successfully in any strange place, your RAS is filtering for ways you can do that.

When you walk into a roomful of people you don't know, if you believe you don't have what it takes to be successful there, your RAS is filtering for danger so you don't come to harm. If you believe you're walking into a personal or professional opportunity, your RAS is filtering for ways you can find it.

> *In each case, your experience is different because your RAS is filtering those two billion bits of data in completely different ways.*

Now that you know about your RAS, can you think of any experiences in which you were aware of that filtering?

My Early Experiences with RAS

When I was in my twenties, I had two significant experiences of my RAS at work, although at the time I was completely ignorant about what it was. In 1971, I was living in New York City with my maternal grandmother for three months, taking care of her after she fell and broke her hip. She lived in an apartment on the Upper East Side, on Madison Avenue, between 88th and 89th Streets, just east of Central Park and just south of Harlem.

In those days, I still believed I was invincible. I'd left my parents' home, made my way in the world, and was now, through a series of negotiations with my parents, who had limited choices for care of my Nana, living in New York City with her. It was a very heady time. Like any nineteen-year-old, I felt free as a bird—completely unaware of my physical limitations as I walked all over the Upper East Side all by myself.

One day I walked up Madison Avenue from 89th Street past 125th Street to go to the Army Navy Store in Harlem to buy a pair of jeans. When my Nana found out what I had done as I told her about my adventure getting my prized Levis, she almost had a heart attack. The Army Navy Store was in the heart of East Harlem. According to my Nana, that's an area where I shouldn't have been safe. As a lifelong resident of the city, she believed that it wasn't possible for an Irish girl like me to go into Harlem and get out alive. She was astounded when I told her that every single person I encountered was kind to me, spoke with me, and helped me, no matter what their race or color.

My guess is that it was my anti-war belief that all of us are connected to each other that shone through in my behavior and was reciprocated by everyone. My RAS was filtering for help to get to the store, and I found that help all along the way.

The second RAS experience that stands out for me happened when I lived near Balboa Park in San Diego several years later. Balboa Park is a beautiful park just a little north of downtown; as beautiful as it is in the daytime, it was very dangerous to be near between sundown and sunrise. I knew of that danger since I lived in an apartment nearby.

As a morning person, I had my greatest energy in the early morning. Moving to San Diego from New York helped me easily get up at 4:30 a.m. and still feel like I was sleeping in until 7:30; in fact, I don't think I ever got off New York time the whole time I lived in California.

Taking up running was one of the ways I channeled my natural adrenaline overload so I could focus on what I had to do that day. Taking my runs on 5th Avenue, right at the edge of Balboa Park, at 4:30 a.m. on weekdays, meant that I could get in a daily run and still get to the submarine dry dock before morning quarters at 7:00 a.m. Each morning as I ran, I had every confidence that I could keep myself safe.

As one of the few women in San Diego who were sandblasting and painting submarines and engaging in docking and un-dockings, along with the distinction of being a graduate of both the Basic and Advanced Firefighting and Damage Control Schools, I believed I had what it took to seem too intimidating for anyone to attack in the early morning hours. Perception is everything—I was one badass chick!

Being almost six feet tall certainly helped me. I looked as mean as possible whenever another human being appeared, stayed hyper-vigilant in all directions, and crossed the street if anyone was walking on the same side of the street I was running on. I also kept to the side of the street across from the park unless I was crossing to avoid someone; then I got right back to it the moment the danger passed. My RAS was filtering for movement in the area and alternative escape routes.

Everyone told me I was taking my life in my hands by being anywhere Balboa Park at that time in the morning. As a twenty-something, I believed that I knew better. Circumstances proved that I did.

Looking back, it's clear that I had lost my anti-war belief that we are all connected, yet my RAS was still filtering my experience in alignment with my beliefs. Nothing ever happened to me when I was running there; once or twice a few early walkers crossed the street to avoid *me*!

Those two incidents stand out in my mind because I could connect my beliefs to my experience. Later on when I was connecting my other beliefs about myself to the experiences I was having, these two situations shone like beacons for me to remember.

What about you? What are your experiences with your RAS?

- Have you ever wanted to win something at a fair—and you did?
- Have you ever believed that a job you wanted was yours—and the interview seemed effortless?
- Have you ever seen a smiling face across a crowded room and in time that person became your best friend or your spouse?

Each of these experiences is the result of your RAS filtering the information you need to be successful.

Take Action

Here's an experiment you can do to get conscious of your RAS: Think about the last car you bought. Had you ever noticed how many of them there were on the road before you bought one? Now you see them everywhere!

Here's how you can watch your RAS at work without having to spend a dime: Think of your dream car—the one you'd buy if money was no object. (Mine is a Baltic Blue Range Rover Evoque.) Get a picture of your dream car out of a magazine or off the internet and hang it up in your office or in your home somewhere. I guarantee you that within twenty-four hours you'll see that car everywhere.

If you'd never heard of the RAS, it would be hard to change your brain filters—your beliefs. Now that you know about it, you can start to use what you're learning in this book to reprogram your brain in a way that helps you create remarkable results in your life.

Now you have a choice. Use what you're learning in this book to program your brain to let in everything that will support you and move you forward in life.

Connecting Your RAS to Your Beliefs

Remember what you read in the last chapter about the process of generating your own beliefs? That is how you make the RAS work for you!

Your family started programming your RAS from the time you were born. The authorities of your childhood—church, school, community—continued the process until you came across a contrary authority or an expert. Then you had to make a decision: Keep your filter on that topic or reprogram your RAS with a new belief.

Your experience changed as your beliefs did. Then you began to generate your own beliefs; you changed the filters in your RAS as you did so. You did it over and over again, although you might never have been conscious of the process.

Let's Review

Everything we've learned about the science of the brain and our beliefs can be summarized in the following simple statements:

1. A belief is something we decide is true.
2. The purpose of the RAS is to keep us safe. We filter our experience through our RAS with our beliefs because that's how we make sense of our world.
3. Filtering our experience with our beliefs allows us to move through our days without having to make a new decision every step of the way. Once we believe something, we've already decided; after that, our RAS does the rest of the work.

4. The filters in our RAS (our beliefs) are constant across all contexts. When you change a belief in one area of your life, that new belief affects every other area of your life.
5. Because of our RAS, our beliefs are the basis of our reality; our beliefs also provide us with the motivation to act.

6. 1st Gear is our subjective experience in any given moment as a result of our beliefs, values, opinions, and experiences.
7. The secret to changing your mind about anything is to be willing to explore your beliefs and reprogram your RAS over time. The good news is that this RAS programming is only as permanent as we want it to be. That's why the Journey to Powerful Presence begins with exploring your beliefs.

Now you know how it works: You can program your RAS to work for you.

Take Action

What do you think about what you just read? Capture your thoughts in your journal.

In the next chapter, we'll explore the RAS on a more personal level as you learn exactly how to consciously engage it.

Dance into Your Power

Chapter 10

Choosing the Three Empowering Beliefs

We've just spent the last two chapters exploring the science of beliefs and our brains. We've almost finished laying the foundation for exploring the Three Empowering Beliefs that are at the heart of Powerful Presence.

Let's Make It Personal

As simple as it is to recognize that:

1. your beliefs about yourself are at the heart of your presence, and
2. your RAS is the structure in your brain to program with positive beliefs when you want to increase the power of your presence,

it still takes time to change your beliefs.

Your RAS is part of your 1st Gear, which can be difficult to change directly since it's composed of all of your beliefs, values, opinions, and experiences. Once you understand how these four are connected, it's much easier to reprogram your RAS.

Here's the process I discovered:

1. When you have an experience that's contrary to a belief you hold, you have the motivation to explore things further, starting with your opinions.
2. Because your opinion about something is based on your subjective experience, it's easier to change your opinion than it is to change your beliefs. Once you've changed your opinion about what's possible, it's even easier to change your behavior.
3. New behavior changes your experience, and *that* gives you the motivation to change your beliefs.

> *Changing your beliefs requires a willingness to change your behavior.*

Behavior is very simple to change as long as you're willing to keep at it. To quote my all-time favorite professor in college, the late Dr. John Wilson, "There's the 'first time' and there's 'perfection'—and these two never happen at the same moment. So give yourself a break and make some mistakes. You'll learn faster."

There's a process for changing your beliefs that I've found to be exceptionally effective on my own Journey. I journal my experiences as they happen; then I periodically go back and see what I learned. Mapped out, the process looks like this:

1. Explore different experiences and *try them on for size*, using all three Gears.
2. Gather the data you obtain from having these new experiences and document it in your journal.

3. Determine how these new experiences affect your opinions; make changes as necessary.
4. Check your new opinions with your values; determine if anything has changed.
5. Update your values as necessary with the new data you have.
6. Check your old beliefs against your new experiences, opinions, and values.
7. Update your beliefs as necessary. Journal what you've learned.

One of the biggest benefits to having three Gears is that you can examine your experiences from three different perspectives. You gather a lot more data that way and you discover things that were invisible to you when you had only 1st Gear.

When you consider your experiences like this, it's like opening a secret back door into your RAS. It gives you the space to examine everything you go through from three different angles so you can determine whether your beliefs about yourself are serving you. When they're not, you can do something about it.

At the heart of your Powerful Presence are the beliefs you have about yourself and your abilities. Examining these beliefs is the first step in getting conscious of your presence—so you can make it powerful.

At this point, it's worth repeating some things we've already said about our beliefs about ourselves. They:

1. form the basis of the ways in which we interact with the world
2. determine whether we feel powerful—or not
3. enter the room before we do

When I first started getting conscious of my beliefs about myself, it was very painful to realize that I didn't have many positive ones.

The positive ones I did have were all about my abilities at work—things I had proved were true simply by being successful at them. For example, I knew I had what it took to sandblast and paint submarines. I knew that I could find any piece of equipment that our ship's company needed to do that job because I had created relationships with every vendor in the area. And I knew I was one of very few women who had the courage—and the opportunity—to complete the Navy's Basic and Advanced Firefighting and Damage Control Schools.

The negative beliefs I held were about my worthiness as a human being. It took my willingness to look at them, and the help of several skilled and compassionate therapists and coaches, before I learned a structure for doing it on my own. Along the way, I learned—and created—strategies that would help me change my beliefs more easily and in less time.

The most exciting thing I learned was that if I wanted to achieve something I didn't know how to do—in my case that was thinking positively about myself—I could find someone else who knew how to do it. Then I could simply do what they were doing! I *acted as if* I were them.

I learned that these people are our *role models*. When you act as if you are them, it skyrockets your ability to transform any negative beliefs you hold. Discovering this was magic for me.

You may have heard the phrase "Fake it till you make it." It's a variation of "Act as if." It's the secret to acting in a way that defies the negative beliefs you've identified about yourself. It's the direct route to increasing the power of your presence and achieving things you never thought possible.

Role Models for Powerful Beliefs

As I was learning to change my beliefs about myself, I had three significant role models: Viktor Frankl, Helen Keller, and Nelson Mandela.

They proved to me that the term *successful* has many different meanings. Each of them lived in different times and had different life experiences, yet they all became famous for the ways in which they overcame the overwhelmingly "negative" circumstances they faced. Each of them taught me the power of being fueled by your inner beliefs—beliefs that are more powerful than your circumstances.

Viktor Frankl

Have you ever heard of Viktor Frankl? You can see him for yourself on YouTube at this link: *http://psyhistorik.livejournal.com/34159.html.*

Mr. Frankl has inspired generations of people in the helping professions, especially those in suicide prevention, addiction recovery, and family therapy.

Viktor Frankl was a twentieth-century Jewish psychologist and neurologist from Vienna, Austria. He used his professional training in suicide prevention when he was a prisoner of the Nazis in World War II to help his fellow concentration camp prisoners survive, for as long as possible, the devastation of that experience.

Despite losing everything he had, including his young wife and his parents, he kept his thoughts focused on the positive meaning of everything that was happening around him. In that way he kept himself, and others, focused on hope instead of despair. Later he wrote about the experience in a book titled *Man's Search for Meaning*, which is still listed on *Amazon.com* as the #1 self-help book ever written. He wrote that he survived because he "found a way out in my mental life—an invaluable opportunity to dwell in the spiritual domain, the one that the SS were unable to destroy."

> *Viktor Frankl believed that* **he brought about what he thought about,** *so he kept his thoughts positive and nourishing.*

Helen Keller

Helen Keller is famous for her belief that she had what it takes to make a difference on the planet despite devastating physical disabilities. When I learned about her life, I was about ten years old, and I saw the movie, *The Miracle Worker*. Meeting her in that movie left a seed in me that blossomed many years later.

Before she was seven, Helen created her own language to communicate with her family despite her triple disabilities of blindness, deafness and a severe speech impediment. Once she started working with Annie Sullivan, the sky was the limit for her. In her writing and her travels around the world, Helen worked tirelessly for people with disabilities. In 1999, she was listed in Gallup's Most Widely Admired People of the 20th Century—thirty-one years after her death.

> *Helen Keller believed that she* **had what it takes** *to accomplish anything.*

Nelson Mandela

On February 11th, 1990, when Nelson Mandela was released from prison after twenty-seven brutal and demeaning years, the event was broadcast live all over the world. Four years later, the seventy-five-year-old Mandela was being sworn in as South Africa's first black president, and everyone in the world knew his name.

Mr. Mandela survived his prison ordeal with the unwavering belief that he was "the captain of [his] ship, the master of [his] fate." No matter how he was treated, and despite everything he lost in the process, no one could shatter his belief in himself and his cause.

People all over the world found out about him when, as president, he used the power of his position to heal the racial wounds of his country. He believed that the obstacles he faced would now be the gifts he brought to his presidency. Since then, Nelson Mandela has won over 250 awards including the 1993 Nobel Peace Prize.

> *Nelson Mandela believed that obstacles* **bring gifts**,
> *so he used those obstacles to gift the world*
> *with freedom for his country.*

The Three Empowering Beliefs

My first three role models started me on the path to uncovering the power of my beliefs about myself.

In the last twenty years, I've learned from many more teachers and role models about that power. When I put together everything I'd learned, I discovered that all of the beliefs we have about ourselves that fuel our Powerful Presence are variations of these three:

1. You bring about what you think about.
2. You have what it takes.
3. There's a gift in every obstacle.

These beliefs are the foundation of Powerful Presence; without them, the Three Resourceful Abilities and Three Focused Actions are not possible.

> *There is no shortcut to Powerful Presence*
> *without these Three Empowering Beliefs.*

The work required to develop these beliefs is worth all the effort it might take, since this is where you begin to discover and develop your unique Powerful Presence. The work you do to explore these

Three Empowering Beliefs for yourself is the first step you take to dance into your own power. Judging by the example of my three role models, when you dance into your own power, your presence becomes powerful—and so does your impact.

Now that we've thoroughly explored the power of the Three Empowering Beliefs, let's investigate them one by one in the next three chapters.

Chapter 11

Belief #1: You Bring About What You Think About

The first time I was exposed to this belief I was a Navy counselor just graduated from training, reporting to my first job at the Counseling and Assistance Center at NAS Cecil Field, Jacksonville, Florida. It was June of 1984.

This was a two-year tour; I was stationed in Florida, unaccompanied by my second husband and without my friends. I was the most junior person on the staff as well as the only woman.

Instead of the job I wanted back at NAS Chase Field in Beeville, Texas, close to my home in Corpus Christi, I was stationed in one of my least favorite places on the planet. To say I was feeling unresourceful would be an understatement.

On my way into the counseling center headquarters to meet with my commanding officer that first Monday morning, I noticed a plaque on the wall. Since I was dragging my feet a bit that day, I stopped to read it. Here's what it said:

> *"That which you can conceive of, believe in and confidently expect, must necessarily become your experience."* —*Paul J. Meyer*

The lightning bolt that hit me right between the eyes as I read this almost knocked me down! I couldn't believe what I'd just read.

Why on earth would there be a quote on the wall that would invite me to make my dearest wish come true? Why on earth would there be a sign on the wall that would point me directly to getting out of here—*before I'd even met my new boss or settled into my new office?*

Although I couldn't let myself completely believe it yet, I copied that quote down on a 3x5 index card as soon as I got into my new office that morning. It was the first thing I put up on my wall.

Over the next several months, as I began my work with my new clients and colleagues, I kept in touch with those I'd left behind at NAS Chase Field. I told them about the quote, that it was hanging on my wall, and that I read it every day.

Within eight months, one of my former colleagues told me that the counselor who'd taken "my" spot at the counseling center in Beeville had begun having problems and was relieved of his duties. He was in the same position I was: half the country away from his wife and friends and feeling isolated and alone. Unlike me, though, he let those feelings overwhelm him so much that it cost him his job.

I'd been reading my motivational index card daily. I seriously believed that if I could just *see* my transfer back to Chase Field in my mind's eye, I could make it happen. Now that there was no one in that job, I believed I could find a way to get back to my home and my friends in Texas.

Because of these beliefs, I set in motion a number of things that resulted in my doing just that—exactly one year after I first read that quote.

By now you know that my RAS was in high gear, helping me identify those things that would help me accomplish my goal—in the same way you can now pick out all the cars that match your dream car as you're driving on the highway. At that point, however, I had no idea that I *had* an RAS.

Even though I only had this one empowering quote to fuel my beliefs, and no knowledge of my RAS, my experience in Florida was life-changing. Here are the events that returned me to Texas:

1. I believed I could get back to NAS Chase Field and I could see it happening. I believed—with all of my heart—that it could be done and that I was just the person to do it.
2. I took action to support my beliefs. The day I got the news about the vacancy, I contacted my former boss at NAS Chase Field to tell her I wanted to help her out by volunteering to fill the now-empty position. She happily accepted my offer and then followed up with her human resources officer in Washington to set the wheels in motion; she requested me by name and shared with him the details of our situation.
3. What helped us out the most with Washington was that I was the junior member of a five-member team in Jacksonville—and NAS Chase Field had an empty counseling center. Without a qualified person to take over that job, my former boss would have had to wait six to eighteen months to get it filled. This constituted a hardship for NAS Chase Field that Washington had every incentive to address now that the officer in charge of the program had reported it, and they supported her request with a solution.

Three things are very clear to me as I look back: I wanted to go back home to Texas, I believed I could do it, and I found a way to make it happen. In the process, I proved the power of Mr. Meyer's belief to myself. More important, it was now mine to use again whenever I needed it.

Using That Belief Again

Four years later, after ending my marriage to my second husband and spending a year "doing my personal work," I knew I wanted to meet someone with whom I could create a successful relationship. I wanted my third marriage to be my last.

On January 1st, 1989, I launched my New Year by claiming my belief in this man's existence. I spoke it out loud, and I spoke it *every single day.*

Remembering how powerful Mr. Meyer's quote had been for me in 1984—when it was only a stunning possibility—kept me going. I'd gotten amazing results from it when I only wanted to believe it; this time I imagined that my results were going to be nothing short of spectacular.

In late November of 1989, I got a call from Chuck Beatty, a geologist at Exxon, who wanted to hire me to bring my stress management program, Stress Arresters, to his team for their end-of-the-year safety meeting on December 19th.

We met on December 19th, 1989. By January 6th, 1990, we'd already had a three-hour lunch and a six-hour first date; I knew he was The One. On October 5th, 1990, we married.

This time I was conscious about my ability to *bring about what I thought about;* I believed it with all my heart. I was willing to pay attention, and then I took action when my opportunity knocked.

The Rest of the Story

The reason I believe that *you bring about what you think about* is because I've done it so many times. With that belief, I've created everything that exists in my life today, including my thriving—twenty-two years and counting—marriage to Chuck. When I was putting together the elements of Powerful Presence, it was clear to me that this belief is the foundation of all of my success. I learned it from Paul J. Meyer, and I made it my own.

As I synthesized everything I'd learned to create the Journey to Powerful Presence, it was clear to me that a lot of other people—many of them famous—had achieved the same results that I had using this belief. Here are some examples from famous people you may have heard of:

- **Dale Carnegie:** "Remember, happiness doesn't depend on who you are or what you have. It depends solely on what you think."
- **Oprah Winfrey:** "You don't become what you want, you become what you believe."
- **Louise L. Hay:** "Whatever we believe becomes true for us."
- **Napoleon Hill:** "You can if you believe you can."

My Powerful Presence role models all acted on this belief as well:

- **Viktor Frankl** thought about hope in the midst of despair. He brought light to thousands of prisoners in the darkness of Nazi concentration camps. He's inspired millions of people to believe in the power of their thoughts through his book about his experience, *Man's Search for Meaning*.
- **Helen Keller** thought about developing every ability possible in the midst of her multiple disabilities. She thought only about *what she could do*; she wasted no time despairing about what she couldn't. She accomplished more in her lifetime than many others who have sight and hearing.

- **Nelson Mandela** thought about ending apartheid in the midst of being imprisoned because of it. Throughout his twenty-seven years in prison, he was undaunted in his belief that he would help end it. Four years later, as the first black president of South Africa, he worked with the man he defeated at the polls to finally dismantle apartheid.

How About You?

In Chapter 8, you learned that your beliefs come from three sources. There's also a structure within which you can change your beliefs, even though it might take some time.

You're now at the point in your Journey to Powerful Presence at which you have a decision to make:

> *Will you try on this new belief using everything you've learned so far to help you?*

Here We Go

Now that you're ready to try on the belief that *you bring about what you think about*, the very first things you're likely to encounter at this point in your Journey are negative beliefs you may hold about yourself.

Remember that your presence is grounded in your beliefs about yourself. When you pay attention to your thoughts, you'll have no trouble identifying the negative beliefs that get in your way. Some of those beliefs may already have surfaced as you read about my role models.

When you start paying attention to what you think about, you'll be surprised by how closely connected your thoughts are to your results. When things don't seem to be going well for my clients, I always recommend that they pay attention to their thoughts. They have found that the connection is direct.

Face Those Negative Beliefs

Once you get conscious of the negative beliefs you hold, you start to reduce the hold they have over you. You begin to change your experience once you accept that these beliefs are simply a part of your 1st Gear, not the absolute truth about you. This knowledge is the door to your freedom from them; now you have a choice about what you want to believe. That choice is your first step in reprogramming your RAS so you can change your experience.

> *Changing your experience is the first step*
> *in changing your beliefs.*

Here are some examples of negative beliefs I've held—and heard about from my clients:

1. I don't have the right [*clothes, contacts, supplies, etc.*] to accomplish [*fill in the blank*].
2. I don't know how to …
3. I tried this before and it didn't work.
4. I'm not that good at [*speaking, networking, dating, cooking, meeting new people, etc.*].
5. I'm too [*fill in the blank*] to [*succeed, move up the ladder at work, find the right mate, etc.*].
6. I'll never deserve to get or do or be [*something positive*].
7. Other people just don't give me a chance to …
8. People who are great at [*fill in the blank*] know something—or have some quality—that I don't.

These are just a few of the common beliefs that create obstacles to your success; the others out there are simply variations on these themes.

When I work with my clients to debunk the negative beliefs that stop them, we use a combination of powerful and quantifying questions that allow them to identify other possibilities they can examine and experience.

Let's look at each of the eight negative beliefs you just read. I've restated them below and included three examples of these powerful and quantifying questions as well as a new empowering belief that will increase your Powerful Presence.

See what you think of the process.

1. **I don't have the right [*clothes, contacts, supplies, etc.*] to accomplish [*fill in the blank*].**
   a. What, specifically, *are* the right clothes, contacts, supplies, etc.?
   b. Where can you get them?
   c. What will it cost you to get them?
   d. *New empowering belief:* Once I know what I need, I go out and get it.

2. **I don't know how to …**
   a. Have you ever done *anything like this* before—anywhere or at any time?
   b. If you've never done it before, who do you know who has? How, specifically, did they do it?
   c. What if you *did* know how?
   d. *New empowering belief:* Once I know what to do, I can do anything. I can learn how to do anything.

3. **I tried this before and it didn't work.**
   a. What, specifically, did you try?
   b. What obstacles did you face? What did you do about them?
   c. What do you know now that you didn't know then?
   d. *New empowering belief:* Every time I try something, I learn something new. I'm successful because I'm willing to try new things more than once.

4. **I'm not that good at [*speaking, networking, dating, cooking, meeting new people, etc.*].**
   a. What have you ever done that's similar?

   b. What are you good at now?
   c. What was the first thing you did to learn it?
   d. *New empowering belief:* I'm already good at [*fill in the blank*] and I can learn to be good at anything else I want to be good at.

5. **I'm too [*fill in the blank*] to [*succeed, move up the ladder at work, find the right mate, etc.*].**
   a. Too [*fill in the blank*] for whom?
   b. What makes her opinion so important to you?
   c. What if you could [*fill in the blank*]?
   d. *New empowering belief:* I have everything I need to [*fill in the blank*] and I'm ready to learn anything else I need to succeed at it. My opinion of me is more important to my success than anyone else's.

6. **I'll never deserve to get or do or be [*something positive*].**
   a. Never?
   b. *Who* says so?
   c. What's your criteria for being deserving or for being worthy of good?
   d. *New empowering belief:* I am worthy of all good things— because I say so. I open my arms to receive all the good that is coming to me.

7. **Other people just don't give me a chance to …**
   a. Which other people? What power do they have over your results?
   b. You have no power over other people, only how you interact with them. What could you do differently?
   c. Who do you know who is successful at what you want to do? What are they doing that you're not doing?
   d. *New empowering belief:* I can learn how to relate to other people successfully.

8. **People who are great at [*fill in the blank*] know something—or have some quality—that I don't.**

a. Who's great at this? *Name names.*

b. What, specifically, do they know — or have — that you don't?

c. What do you need to do to learn what they know or develop that quality?

d. *New empowering belief:* Once I identify anything I want to do or have, I have what it takes to do what's necessary to claim it for myself.

Take Action

Before you read any further, take a moment to digest what you've just read. In your journal, capture the thoughts and feelings you are having right now. They will be an important indicator of your progress as you travel further on your Journey.

What did you think of the process? Did you feel the difference between the old disempowering belief and the new empowering one? You might even have felt it physically.

Investigating your beliefs like this is the first stop on your Journey to Powerful Presence. You're exploring here. It's important to take some time and give it your attention.

When you discover an old belief that no longer serves you, here's a three-step process for transforming it:

Step 1. **Say it out loud.** That's the first step to increasing your awareness. You can change any of your old beliefs once you identify them.

Step 2. **Question the belief.** Ask yourself, "Is this really true from an objective 3rd Gear, or is this something I learned a long time ago that's now outdated?"

Step 3. **Create an alternative belief to try on, as if it were a piece of clothing.** Believing anything requires the experience of using it, so give yourself the time to practice with it. Adjust the new belief as necessary until you're getting the results you want.

> ┌─ **Take Action** ─────────────────────────────
>
> Using your journal to record your progress, claim three of the empowering beliefs above and play with them for the next thirty days. First, identify the negative beliefs you have that have prevented you from using these beliefs before now, and then create your own version of the process you saw above:
>
> 1. Negative belief, 2. Qualifying questions, 3. New empowering belief.

Why Does This Work?

We're talking about personal power here. The reason these strategies work, 100 percent of the time, is because you're developing your power in the only place it's guaranteed: *inside yourself*. You're dancing into your power now, one step at a time.

You have no power over circumstances, only over your response to them. You only have power over your own thoughts and your willingness to connect those thoughts to your results. You create the dance steps that work for you. You program your RAS to help you create your own dance when you believe that *you bring about what you think about*.

- When you hold this belief, you're more likely to pay attention to your thoughts when you don't get the results you want.
- Paying attention allows you to adjust—now you have a choice. When you have a choice, you're not stuck.
- When you're not stuck, you can move.
- If you can move, you can dance.

Let's put this in perspective for a moment. The alternative to believing that *you bring about what you think about* is thinking that *you're a victim of your circumstances*. There's no hope for you with this disempowering belief; your results are certain to be dismal.

Let's Look at the Research

My background is in psychology and communication. I've also been trained in addictions recovery. In the course of my training, several of my instructors told stories to illustrate behavioral points.

One of the stories I heard all those years ago is the perfect illustration of believing that you bring about what you think about. This story is about two psychologists researching the parameters of optimism and pessimism. Here's my version of it:

Two psychologists decided to discover the root cause of optimism and pessimism. They wanted to prove that both of these patterns of thinking were unconnected to circumstances. The hypothesis they set out to investigate was this: Do you bring about what you think about; i.e., can true optimism and true pessimism be affected by circumstances?

In psychological research, it's critical to isolate the elements you're investigating so you can be sure that the relationships you think exist actually do, and are not affected by something outside of your experiment. In order to be sure that the optimism and pessimism of their subjects was not the result of life circumstances, the psychologists decided to work with children.

After going through all the proper procedures and protocols to ensure the complete safety of the children with whom they'd be working, the psychologists identified two boys as their subjects. Both were about ten years old, and it just so happened that they lived on opposite sides of the same town. Both were the only child of their parents. After months of preparation, they were ready for their experiment at 9:00 a.m. on a sunny Sunday morning.

The first boy was the son of a business owner and his wife. Although he was dearly loved and had every advantage, he was famous for his pessimism. His name was Billy.

The psychologists took him to the amusement park in town with his parents. They told him that everything had been arranged for him to have the park to himself all morning, since it didn't open to the public until noon. His parents smiled in approval and told him to go with the psychologists and do what they asked him to do. Mom and Dad would be waiting outside the gate for him and they would all go to lunch afterwards and talk about his adventure.

The psychologists took Billy to the center of the park and sat him down on one of the benches there. They pointed to everything around them and told him that the entire park was available to him; all of the rides were open and everyone there was ready to give him anything he wanted at any of the concession stands. He could eat anything and play with anything. He could have any toys he wanted. All had been arranged so that anything he wanted was already paid for; everything he wanted was already his. The psychologists told Billy they'd be back for him in a couple of hours and invited him to have a wonderful time.

Two hours later, when they came back to the center of the park, the psychologists found Billy exactly where they'd left him. He was sitting on the same bench, head down, swinging his legs and looking at his shoes. There were no toys or candy near him and no evidence that he had been on any of the rides. It looked as if he hadn't moved from that spot.

One of the psychologists asked, "Billy, is everything OK?" Billy said that it was.

The other one asked, "Did you have any fun?" Billy said everything was fine.

The first one asked him if he had enjoyed any of the rides or eaten any food. Billy said, "No, I thought it would be better to stay put. I didn't want to break any toys or get sick on any of the rides. I didn't want to get a stomachache before lunch with my parents, and I didn't want to get lost. I couldn't think of anything good that would happen if I did what you said, so I just stayed here."

The psychologists told Billy that he had helped them very much and they brought him right to his parents, who took him out to lunch.

Then the psychologists left for the home of the second boy, Charlie, whose parents ran a very successful farm. Charlie was famous for his optimism, and had been since his parents brought him home from the hospital. His nickname was "Sunny Charlie."

Both psychologists, Charlie, and Charlie's parents walked over to a large barn on the edge of the property that had been specially prepared for this experiment. It was filled, wall to wall and floor to ceiling, with a solid mound of horse manure.

Next to the open door, there were three items: a shovel, a pail and a rake. The older of the two psychologists said to Charlie, "There's a big mess in there, Charlie, and it's up to you to clean it up. Your parents will be coming with us and we'll be back in a few hours to make sure you've completed your work."

His parents looked at him solemnly and walked off with the two psychologists.

Two hours later, they all came back. Before they got to the entrance of the barn, they heard some off-key humming followed by a scraping sound. The humming and scraping followed an offbeat rhythm; both were slightly muffled.

When they got to the open door of the barn, all they could see was a Charlie-sized tunnel through the manure. All four mouths dropped open. They were even more astonished when they saw a number of pail-sized piles of manure at the side of the barn.

His mother called out, "Charlie?!"

A perky voice answered, "Yes, Mama!"

The older psychologist asked, "Charlie, are you all right?" Charlie said that he was.

Then his father asked, "Charlie, what are you doing, Son?"

Charlie said, "Well, Papa, there's so much manure in here, I know *there's got to be a pony!*"

Of course the two psychologists proved their theory that you bring about what you think about. Each child had the particular experience he had because of his thoughts, not his circumstances.

The RAS makes *bringing about what you think about* so easy that a child can do it. And we've all been doing it since we were children because…

> *Humans are hard-wired to bring about*
> *what we think about!*

Remember the RAS

You discovered the RAS in the last chapter. Now you know that there's a part of your brain called the reticular activating system (RAS) that filters information for you so you can make sense of your surroundings and your experiences.

If you're still wondering how this could be true, think about what you just read about Billy's experience at the amusement park and Charlie's experience in the barn. What made the difference between them?

> *Billy was filtering for disaster and*
> *Charlie was filtering for fun.*

That's it.

Billy couldn't enjoy a gift horse if you handed it to him; he'd be afraid that he'd fall off it or that the horse would bite him. Charlie, on the other hand, was undaunted by the fact that his parents walked off with two strangers and left him to shovel out an entire barn full of horse manure!

I was taught that resilience is a choice; the story of the optimist and the pessimist is an illustration of how each of these choices worked. I've never forgotten the impact this story had on me. For the last twenty years, my clients and I have benefitted mightily from looking for the pony in the midst of life's inevitable manure. (More on this in Belief #3.)

There's one important distinction I've discovered since I first heard that story. My clients always ask me if some people are simply hard-wired to be like Billy and will always be pessimists. That's a great question.

In my experience over the last thirty years of doing this work with myself and my clients, one thing has consistently proven to be the ultimate antidote to pessimism: the willingness to try new behavior. If Billy had been my client, I would have suggested that he try some exploring despite his misgivings. If he had found something he liked, it would have affected his experience. A new toy, a fun ride or something good to eat would have contradicted his 1st Gear — his current truth about reality. More experiences like that would have helped him shift his outlook.

Remember my role-model strategy? When you "act as if" something positive is true, you reprogram your RAS to filter for different data. Teaching Billy to "act as if" he was Charlie would have helped him learn to create different results. The reason I love this story is that

I've been Billy—and I was taught to think like Charlie. Transferring that knowledge to my clients has been the secret of my success.

So how can you use all of this to consciously think about what you want to bring about?

You have to catch yourself thinking—and you have to have a strategy to help you adjust your thoughts.

The Clock Face Technique

This strategy will help you shift from a negative thought to a positive one so you can identify the particular thoughts that will bring you the most positive results. It's a variation of a technique I learned in the mid-nineties in a course on Neurolinguistic Programming (NLP), which you may remember is the study of the structure of experience.

In that class we learned that you can use your imagination—along with all of your senses—to shift your emotional state from negative to positive. In doing so, you can create the kind of positive emotional state that allows your brain to function at the peak of its powers, because you've reprogrammed your RAS to filter for something else.

Since a strong enough positive thought will dismantle a negative one, the goal here is to find the positive thought that will shift you out of being "stuck" and into being "in action."

The Clock Face Technique is a strategy you can practice yourself to see this shift in your own life. In order to make this true-to-life for you so you can experience it in your 1st Gear, think of a situation in which you were stuck in a negative state. When you read the description that follows, think about a specific situation so you can identify what you might have been thinking at the time.

CAUTION: First read the technique below and the example that follows before you try to use it. Once you understand how the technique works, use the steps that follow it to shift your thinking and see what happens.

The Clock Face Technique

1. Imagine you're standing at 12 o'clock on a huge clock face that lies on the floor in front of you. You're facing 6 o'clock; 3 o'clock is on your left and 9 o'clock is on your right.
2. Your mission at 12 o'clock is to simply stand there and fully experience the negative thoughts and feelings you have about this particular situation: What do you see, feel, and hear? What are you telling yourself right now? What do you believe about yourself right now?
3. Feel your feelings thoroughly. As you stand there at 12 o'clock, try to increase the intensity of your feelings by turning up the volume of anything you're saying or hearing and increasing the intensity of anything you're envisioning in your mind's eye.
4. Once you've got your feelings cranked up to their limit, look straight ahead of you at the space at 6 o'clock and ask yourself, *"Who* would have the *exact opposite* of this feeling?" (Don't worry if it's ridiculous; the funnier, the better, and the more outrageous, the better.)
5. Identify that person—someone you know well, a famous person, a fictional character, or even the animal or cartoon character who embodies the opposite of your previous feeling. Once you've got it, walk straight over to 6 o'clock and step into that person or character, as if you could pull them on like a suit. Pull that "suit" up all around you; immerse yourself in it. Stay facing the direction you're facing, with your back to 12 o'clock.
6. Spend some time in this new state. What do you see, hear, say, and feel now as you become the one who personifies this exact opposite? Revel in the experience with all of your senses and enjoy yourself. See how much you can crank this

one up. What does this person, animal, or character believe about herself right now?

7. When you feel like you're full of this new positive feeling, turn around and walk right back to 12 o'clock. Now turn around once more so you can see 6 o'clock again. This time personify whomever you became when you were standing on 6 o'clock.

8. Now try to remember what you were thinking at 12 o'clock when you first started this technique. What's your impression of it now? (Your experience may vary from slightly shifted out of the negative to completely shifted; it depends on how deeply invested you've been in the original negative belief.)

9. If you find that you have not completely shifted your feelings, you need to go back to 6 o'clock and immerse yourself in that positive experience again. Go back and forth as many times as you need to (it will typically be three times or less) until the negative belief has dissolved and you have a new positive belief that will get you into action.

10. Odds are high that you know exactly what to do now. Do it!

When you're learning a new behavior, it's often useful to have an example from real life. What follows is an example from one of my live classes about someone whose powerfully negative emotion was keeping her from doing something she very much wanted to do. Although this example might seem a bit intense at first, I include it because it's so descriptive of the power of the Clock Face Technique.

1. My client set up her clock face on the floor of our classroom with the other members of the class as witnesses.

2. Her negative emotional state was brought on by the thought that she had to buy a new car. She believed that she was going to get "raped" in the deal. It's often the case when a woman goes by herself to buy a car that she feels at a disadvantage because she's dealing with a man; most car salesmen are male. Oddly enough, the term *raped* is casually

used in the context of car buying and other sales. In this woman's case, that belief had an overwhelming physical impact.

3. Standing at 12 o'clock, her physiology was one of abject fear. She lost the color in her face, she hunched her shoulders up around her ears, and she clenched her teeth and balled her fists. The atmosphere in the room became so thickly negative that the witnesses reported later that they had trouble breathing. No one made a sound as she physically inhabited her fear.

4. When she was ready to identify the person, animal, or cartoon character who held the exact opposite belief, she identified Donald Trump. She was positive that The Donald would walk into any car dealership and get exactly what he wanted at the price he wanted. He would be completely ruthless with any car salesmen he met.

5. As soon as my client identified her opposite, she let out a laugh and headed directly to 6 o'clock.

6. We watched her embody The Donald. Her skin color warmed up, her shoulders relaxed, and she started to swagger. Her voice got hard and she got loud as she started speaking. "I want what I want right now. And if you can't meet my terms, I'll find someone else who will!" We were all laughing and enjoying ourselves as she embodied The Donald buying a car.

7. After several minutes at 6 o'clock, my client headed back to 12 o'clock with a swagger and turned and faced the direction from which she had come. She stood there for a moment, then her shoulders went up a little higher and her voice got a little softer. As soon as she felt the difference, she headed straight back to 6 o'clock, and "Donald Trumped it" for a bit longer. Then she headed back to 12 o'clock and let out a long breath.

8. She reported this time that although she remembered her previous feelings of helplessness and fear, *she didn't feel them*. Her breathing was even and relaxed, even though she was no longer acting like The Donald. Her head was high,

her shoulders were relaxed, and her voice was steady. Her cheeks were a little pink.

9. She said she knew exactly what she needed to do: play two car salesmen against each other! She would go into the two dealerships in her town and simply get information about the car she wanted. She would pay attention to how she was treated. She was prepared to "Trump it" if she had to. She was prepared to walk out if she didn't get exactly what she wanted.

10. My client completed this exercise laughing, head up and shoulders back, to a standing ovation from the class. None of us will ever forget the experience.

11. When she came back to class a few weeks later, she reported that one of the two salesmen had not only met all of her requirements, he had added a few extras on her new car that she hadn't known about and for which she didn't have to pay extra. She felt confident that she had found a salesman she could trust—someone from whom she would buy again. The other salesman had been challenging to deal with until she walked out of the dealership while he was in the middle of a sentence telling her what she couldn't have. She told us that walking out while he was still talking made her feel exceptionally powerful.

What made the difference in this woman's real-life experience? She changed her belief about what was possible and what she was capable of. Then she identified a course of action and took it. *She brought about what she thought about*, and she made believers out of the rest of her classmates.

Now that you know how *you bring about what you think about* works, you're one step closer to using it yourself. What will you do with what you've learned? Here's a strategy to get you started:

1. Pay attention to what you're thinking on a regular basis. Identify your positive and negative beliefs and journal what you find.

2. When you get a result you don't want, check your beliefs. What's another possibility? (Use the Clock Face Technique when you need to.)
3. Connect your outcome to your beliefs and adjust as necessary.

Now that you know that *you bring about what you think about,* you're ready to explore Belief #2 of Powerful Presence: You have what it takes. That's the topic of the next chapter.

Chapter 12

Belief #2: You Have What It Takes

The first time I encountered this belief, I didn't recognize it.

When you were little, did you watch the movie *The Wizard of Oz* with your family? So did I—and I often use the characters and situations from that movie in my coaching and training because of the impact it's had on me since my childhood.

Do you remember that song the Cowardly Lion sings when he and Dorothy and the Tin Man and Scarecrow have gotten all cleaned up in Oz and are getting ready to meet the Wizard? "If I Were King of the Forest" is one of the songs that have stirred the hearts of children of all ages since *The Wizard of Oz* debuted in 1939.

If you want to see Bert Lahr as the Lion sing it again, you can find a clip of this song on YouTube at this link: *www.youtube.com/ watch?v=EPP6L1_ooaQ*

Although I saw this movie every year as I was growing up, loving that song and the transformation it brings to the formerly cowardly Lion, I never recognized it as the sign of a life-changing belief until one significant moment many years later. It was while I was attending a year-long leadership program as part of my coach training in the heart of redwood country just outside San Francisco. Our leadership group met for quarterly retreats with our trainers four or five days each time. We stayed in a gorgeous retreat center called The Mothertree.

One of the larger components of our curriculum was a ropes course, an experiential learning format that involves both low- and high-risk elements in a physically safe and supportive environment. The low-risk elements range from "on the ground" to eight feet above ground; the high-risk elements are eight feet and higher in the air.

One of the first elements we tackled in our ropes course—during the first day of our first retreat—involved climbing twenty-five feet up the side of a redwood tree.

I tried to prepare myself to follow my colleagues and climb up those twenty-five feet. From where I was standing it looked like a thousand feet up. I watched them each shimmy up the tree, climb onto a narrow platform and maneuver around its girth from back to front, then walk out on a plank that stuck out ten feet from the tree trunk into space.

Then, as if climbing all that way and walking out that far into space were not enough, once they got to the edge of the plank they *flung themselves* into midair to catch a trapeze that was hanging about six feet away from the edge of the plank.

I was fifty-two years old. The sight before my eyes was so daunting that my heart was pounding, my breathing was shallow, and my brain was going numb.

Then something interesting began to happen. I heard Bert Lahr's Lion voice in my head—first quietly, then with increasing volume, and in stereo, as I waited my turn at the back of the line for over thirty minutes, watching my colleagues do something that I'd never imagined—in a million years!—would be my fate to attempt.

Finally, it was my turn. By now I was feeling like a huge jungle cat. I had focused so strongly on the Bert-the-Lion-singing-in-my-head that I had hypnotized myself to roar instead of faint. That roar helped me focus on my lion-ness instead of the weakness I felt for being over fifty, six feet tall, and totally out of shape.

As I climbed, endlessly, all the way up that redwood, all the teams in the forest heard me. Once I covered that first twenty feet, I somehow maneuvered myself onto the platform, climbed around the trunk, and made my way out onto the edge of the plank.

Roaring.

Finally, I closed my eyes and *flung* myself out towards the trapeze with the hugest roar of all—then hit the open air and felt my harness being caught by those on the ground as they safely lowered me down the ropes.

Just like the Cowardly Lion, I recognized that courage isn't the absence of fear. It's taking action in spite of your fear and trusting that you have what it takes to get through. Decades apart, the Lion and I proved our royalty in the forest—and everyone heard us.

How About You?

Odds are high that you have your own story of overcoming a fear and discovering that you have what it takes. When you have a huge moment like that, you never forget it, do you?

Take Action

Take a moment and record in your journal any experience you remember that involved your breaking through some fear or mental barrier in a way that surprised you when you did it.

Belief #2 of Powerful Presence takes these experiences one step further. Instead of surprising yourself in a profoundly emotional standout experience, you take it for granted that *you have what it takes* to do anything you want. You have a calm assurance about yourself that allows you to handle anything that shows up. More important, you believe it most of the time.

In case this belief seems incredible to you, let's take a moment to break it down into manageable practices that are easier to digest.

Breaking It Down

Remember we said in Chapter 8 that a belief is simply something you've decided is true?

When you believe that:

1. *you bring about what you think about,*
2. your RAS is filtering for all the data available that matches your beliefs, and
3. your beliefs structure your experience,

you open yourself up to the possibility that many other things could be true as well.

The belief that *you bring about what you think about* opens the door to your Powerful Presence. Belief #2—that *you have what it takes*—allows you to explore the possibility that there's more to you than you suspected.

During my experience on the ropes course, there was something deep inside of me that came to my rescue. It wasn't logical—and it wasn't new. It was something that had inspired me as a child; it was right there, inside me, when I needed it.

How about you? In your experience of overcoming something that seemed insurmountable, where did you get the courage to do it? Odds are high that it came from deep inside of you, too.

It's not just us. How did my Powerful Presence role models do it?

- How did Viktor Frankl survive the horror of the Nazis and save as many people as he did?
- How did Helen Keller overcome the darkness of her blindness and the silence of her deafness to inspire generations of people all across the world?
- How did Nelson Mandela rise above the humiliation of being treated like some despicable beast—separated from everything and everyone he loved for twenty-seven years?

Twentieth-century American author and businessman Bruce Barton says it best: each one of them believed "that something deep inside of them was far superior to circumstances." They believed that they had what it takes to accomplish their desires. More than that, they acted on their belief.

What Gets in the Way?

In the course of learning the strategies of Powerful Presence, one of the biggest challenges my clients face is overcoming a deeply held contrary belief that they'd better not "get too big for their britches." They've been taught by their early authorities to stay small; they've been taught that getting "bigger than they ought to be" will cause them harm. They've been trained like baby elephants!

Have you heard how they train baby elephants to work for humans, either in a circus or as pack animals in Asia? This behavioral strategy has been practiced for thousands of years to dominate an animal that could crush a human in a second. The point of the training is to have the elephant *believe* that the human is more powerful—that the elephant's life is at risk if it disobeys the trainer. In order for the human-elephant connection to work, the elephant must believe in its weakness instead of its strength.

When a wild baby elephant is captured, it is handled roughly, beaten, and yelled at. Then it is tied, inescapably, with ropes. Even at two days old, the baby will thrash to get away. The humans make sure the elephant stays tied securely until it stops fighting and becomes docile. No food, no water, and repeated abuse finally break the baby elephant and it becomes resigned to its fate. This can take a week or more.

Once the baby elephant passes this first stage of its training, and all its resistance ceases, they begin the next phase of its training. This time, the baby elephant is tied with a heavy chain around its front leg so its human can continue teaching it the things it needs to learn to be useful to humans, and so other humans will be safe around it.

As the training continues, most elephants become permanently resigned to their fate; now they can be tied with only a rope. They won't test the strength of the rope against their own even though they could pull down everything around them and crush every human who comes near them. They believe they can't break free, so they never attempt it.

Even an elephant will **bring about what it thinks about.**

What beliefs have you held about yourself that have kept you chained like a baby elephant? Do your beliefs about yourself move you forward to success or hold you back in fear or discouragement?

Take Action

Take a moment and journal your thoughts about what keeps you chained right now.

Where Does This Leave Us?

As the result of believing that *I have what it takes* for all these years, I have been liberated from my own chains, and I've made it my life's work to use Powerful Presence to liberate others. In the process, I've discovered that there are three negative behaviors that stand in the way of believing that *you have what it takes*:

1. comparing yourself to anyone else
2. confusing the desire for something with the experience required to achieve it
3. measuring yourself with anyone else's yardstick

There are also very compelling reasons that each one of these negative behaviors must be released and overcome so you can achieve that liberation. I've had the great fortune to have been helped to do that by three exceptional teachers.

Negative Behavior #1: Comparing Yourself to Anyone Else

I used to compare myself to other people all the time. When I was growing up, I was asked the same question that many people are asked by their frustrated parents in the aftermath of some discovered shortcoming: "Why can't you be more like [*somebody else*]?"

When our often well-meaning parents compared us with our siblings, our neighbors, or our classmates, we were the ones who were lacking in the comparison. So instead of receiving their intended message of a desired improvement, we simply learned to compare ourselves to others. In the process, we learned to focus on our failures instead of our victories. Like those baby elephants, we also learned to focus on our weaknesses instead of our strengths.

Mary Kay Ash changed my beliefs about comparison when I was a Mary Kay consultant for three years in the mid-nineties when we lived in Austin, Texas. Being a Mary Kay consultant in Texas while Mary Kay was still alive was an amazing experience since Mary Kay built her company in Dallas, Texas. Although I'd become a consultant because I believed it was the only way to remain self-employed, the experience transformed my self-image in innumerable ways.

Mary Kay was a woman who proved without a doubt that she had everything it takes to build a multi-billion-dollar company from the ground up, in 1963 — a time when women were not taken seriously in business — or anywhere else. After rising to the top in several sales organizations, she found herself training more men who then became her supervisors than she cared to count. Realizing that this would never change, she left the company she worked for and created her own.

Mary Kay created a company that has developed the highest number of women millionaires in history.

- Her #1 strategy was to build their confidence from the inside out by reminding them, daily, that they had what it takes to be successful in business.
- Her #2 strategy was to teach them everything else they needed to replicate her sales success.
- Her #3 strategy was to reward them for being as spectacular as she believed they were — and they simply proved her right.

Mary Kay had a saying that changed my perception of myself: "Every flower has its own beauty." She'd often say, "Do you think that God compares the daisy to the rose? Each one has its own time and its own beauty. Each one is equally loved by God."

Although it took a while, she helped me change the way I thought about myself — and that changed my business and my personal results.

As a beauty consultant, my success depended on my ability to help other women with their skin care and make-up. This was a daunting task for someone who'd been taught that although she was very smart, she was "no beauty." My beliefs about myself—and my lack of every feminine trait—made my first six months in the business a challenge every day.

As a child I had often been compared to my "prettier" sisters in a less-than-flattering way. I developed a belief that although I did have some fine qualities, beauty was not among them. So selling beauty was a stretch for me.

That's when Mary Kay taught me that just like every flower, "Every woman has her own beauty." I had to find my own beauty before I could help other women find theirs. Finding it was a huge breakthrough that eventually demolished my willingness to compare myself to anyone else. I finally believed that I was completely unique—just like everyone else on the planet.

Mary Kay Ash taught me this: Comparison is a lie.

Take Action

Take a few moments to capture your thoughts about comparisons in your journal. In what ways do you compare yourself to others? How could you begin to put the idea that comparison is a lie into practice?

Negative Behavior #2: Confusing Your Desire for Something with the Experience Required to Achieve It

Just because you want to achieve something that you've never done before doesn't mean that you'll accomplish it perfectly the first time you try it. Malcolm Gladwell made that point in his book *The Outliers*. He says that proficiency is the result of 10,000 hours of doing something!

As the accomplished adults we are, we often forget that learning something new always requires that we be willing to be ignorant at the beginning. Being ignorant simply means that you *know* that you don't know anything. If you're willing to put in the time it takes to get proficient at it, you can increase your skill at anything you want to do.

Twelve years ago, when I was a new gardener, I had no idea what it would take to create the kind of garden I'd been dreaming about for decades. When I started, my only experience was with houseplants, and I had never grown a flower in my life.

What got me out into my first plot of land (the postage-stamp variety, full of red clay, which came with our newly built townhome in northern Virginia) was the belief that garden plants couldn't be that different from potted plants, and that somehow my full-hearted desire for this garden would stand me in good stead. Although I knew I might have to learn some new techniques and strategies, I completely believed that I had what it takes to be a gardener.

From the vantage point of hindsight, I'm clear that this belief was the only thing that got me through the countless mistakes I had to make to get the experience I needed to earn the title of "gardener."

Wanting to have a garden was one thing—my desire for the garden of my dreams allowed me to take a leap of faith and jump in with both feet; in my blissful ignorance, I didn't know what I didn't know. Getting out there and doing the work was another thing entirely—pretty soon it was obvious how much I didn't know and how many mistakes I had to make. I had no idea how hard those first three years of gardening would be—or how much I would learn.

There are two sayings that got me through the effort it required to move from desire to experience in those first three years. The first one comes from my communications professor, Dr. John Wilson: "There's the 'first time' and there's 'perfection'—and these two never happen at the same moment. So give yourself a break and make some mistakes. You'll learn faster."

That helped me remember that I had to put in the time it took to get skilled enough for my garden to exist.

The second saying comes from Tom Hanks in the movie *A League of Their Own*: "If it was easy, everyone would do it." That helped me remember that part of having what it takes to accomplish something is the willingness to stretch yourself and do things that aren't easy. It's the 95 percent perspiration that fuels the 5 percent inspiration; you've got to be willing to sweat sometimes to get what you want.

My garden taught me this: There's a difference between desire and experience.

Take Action

Take a few moments to capture your thoughts in your journal. Do you expect your desire to be enough to accomplish what you want to? How could you begin to put the idea that you need to develop your experience into practice?

Negative Behavior #3: Measuring Yourself with Anyone Else's Yardstick.

When you were a child, did your parents ever stand you up against a door frame or the edge of a wall to measure you as you grew? If they did, you got used to "being measured" before you could count!

Once we got to school, we all experienced the process of being measured. Now it wasn't just our height, it was our prowess in the subjects we were studying and the manner in which we behaved. The letters of the alphabet labeled the kind of students we were. An A student was better than a B student, who was better than a C student. We quickly learned which we were, based on the assessment of our teacher.

In addition to our letter grades, we were also measured in our behavior, which either fit with the norm or did not. Fitting was good. We were being taught how to get along with others and "fit" into society; few of us were taught how to think for ourselves, much less to measure ourselves.

Our parents' and our teachers' assessments were our first measuring sticks. Sometimes those measurements were helpful and sometimes they were not.

My experience with measuring was that I never "measured up." By the time I was in third grade, I was convinced that I was *never* going to measure up. On the outside, it looked like I'd stopped trying; on the inside, I kept measuring myself with other people's yardsticks, believing I didn't have what it took to accomplish much.

For many years, I was caught between the measurements I thought other people were making of me and the measurements I was making of myself. All found me lacking.

What turned this around for me was the help of a very skilled therapist, Dr. Mary Lou Holt, in Corpus Christi, Texas. We worked together for several years in the mid-1980s.

In our work together, she'd always point me back to myself. She taught me the difference between an *outside focus*—with which I look for the information I need from other people, and an *inner focus*—with which I look for what I need within myself. This was hard work. It took me a while to learn to shift—and it changed my life.

Mary Lou taught me the importance of developing criteria for myself—of creating my own standards and measurements based on my own opinions and requirements. First, I had to explore my own opinions and allow myself to expand my experiences so I could decide for myself.

In the process, we discovered that I was judging myself using other people's measurements because I simply wanted their approval. Since I'd felt disapproved of for so long, my strongest need was for someone important to me to approve of me. It never occurred to me that my approval of myself would be the most potent outcome of our work together.

The connection that Dr. Holt helped me make was this: Measuring myself with other people's yardsticks so they will approve of me is a losing game. I can't possibly be sure that they will continue to approve of me or be consistent in how they are measuring me. Some may approve of things in me that others disapprove of; there's simply no way to keep track of the trends. Even if there were, it would exhaust all of my energy.

Instead of relying on anyone else's measurements, Mary Lou taught me to create my own. She taught me that this is an iterative process; it changes and grows as I do. Most important, she taught me that this is the only way that I have any power over my feelings and my experiences; it's the only way I can grow.

As usual, this practice is useful for people other than me. History has proved that my role models used their own yardsticks in the times in which they lived. What would have happened if they hadn't?

- If Viktor Frankl had measured himself using the Nazis' yardstick, he'd have seen himself as merely a Jew who needed to be annihilated to cleanse the world for the Master Race.
- If Helen Keller had measured herself using the yardstick of the society of her time, she'd have seen herself as a deaf, dumb, and blind member of the weaker sex who had no hopes of marrying, let alone leading a fulfilling life.
- If Nelson Mandela had measured himself using the yardstick of apartheid, he'd have seen himself as less than a human being. He couldn't have seen any prospects for his life or for the lives of anyone of his race.

Imagine the loss this world would have suffered if any one of them had not had their own yardstick!

Other people's yardsticks are none of our business. It's our own measurements of ourselves that transform our lives—and inspire the world.

Dr. Holt taught me this: The truest
measure of yourself comes from inside.

Take Action

Take a few moments to capture your thoughts in your journal. Do you use other people's yardsticks to measure yourself? How could you begin to put into practice the idea that your own yardstick is the best measure of your worth?

Now It's Your Turn

Remember the idea from Chapter 11 that you have to catch yourself thinking in order to successfully harness Belief #1 of Powerful Presence: *You bring about what you think about?*

The same is true when you want to develop Belief #2. Although it will certainly get you started, it's not enough to read about my experiences with it, or even to see the effect it had on the lives of my three role models. In order to make it yours, you have to take it out for a spin yourself.

To make that easier for you, here are two strategies that have helped me very much on my Journey. And since 2009, when new Dancers began taking the twelve-week Journey to Powerful Presence, these strategies have also helped them on theirs.

Strategy #1: Take Inventory

This strategy is one I've adapted for my clients from one of the first things Gwen Nichols asked me to do. During our first visit, when I told her that my whole life was a mess and I wanted her to fix it, she told me that she wasn't sure yet if she could. She said it would take both of us to do that job. She asked me to take the time to look in my eyes in the mirror—for just ten seconds a day, each day—before I came back to see her at the end of the week. If I could do that, then she was confident we could fix my life—together.

My first reaction to her suggestion was not positive. "I just paid you $25 and you want me to go home and look at my eyes in the mirror? You've got to be kidding!" Although I didn't say it out loud, I'm sure Gwen saw it all over my face. Despite my initial response, I knew that I really had only two strategies at this point—suicide or doing what she told me to do—so I went home and tried it.

It turned out that I had the perfect place in my little apartment to begin this work: the bathroom. Along with the mirror, it had three other things that were crucial to my success: a lock on the door, a garbage can (great for security), and a light switch. So in I went, ready to give it a try.

It was clear to me that this practice required preparation. I locked the door and put the garbage can up against the door—I lived alone, but I needed that feeling of security. I positioned myself in front of the mirror and began a windup that looked a lot like a pitcher getting ready to throw a fastball. Finally I stopped in front of the mirror, eyes wide open, and counted to ten as fast as I could. Done!

It only took me six weeks to turn the light on.

Yes, I have to admit that it took me a while to look at myself in the bathroom mirror with the light on. Even so, for that first six weeks and for months afterward, I looked in the mirror every day. Eventually the practice transformed me. Now I have a friend in every mirror I walk by—and it's exhilarating. Before that was possible, Gwen had to introduce me to myself so we could work together to heal my life.

Using this strategy will introduce you to yourself, too. It will give you an idea of how you've programmed your RAS. Like Charlie in the barn and Billy in the amusement park, you can only see what you believe is there. Have you programmed your RAS to filter for your strengths? Using this strategy will help you do that.

Looking at yourself in the mirror also gives you the chance to compare what you see in yourself with what someone who loves you sees in you. Those who love you have a filter that allows them to see your strengths. When you can't see them in yourself, you need someone else to help you discover them, just like Gwen helped me to do. Once you've seen your strengths through the eyes of someone who loves you, you can start to reprogram your RAS to filter for them.

This is different from comparing yourself to others. In this strategy, you're comparing how you see yourself with the way someone who loves you sees you. Doing that allows you to discover the strengths in yourself that you may be overlooking.

In my mid-thirties, it became clear to me that, like any captured baby elephant, I saw only my weaknesses. Once I realized this, I knew I needed to ask the people I trusted to help me see what they saw. I discovered that just because I couldn't see my strengths didn't mean they weren't there. This strategy helped me look for them; over time my strengths became much easier to find.

Caution: *This strategy works best when you take the time you need to complete Step 1 (below) with yourself, and then have a private conversation to work through the other two steps with someone who loves you.*

Step 1. Go into your bathroom and close the door. Lock it so you won't be disturbed. Look in your eyes in the mirror for ten seconds. Do this as many times as you need to until you can hold your own gaze for ten seconds. What do you see? Take an inventory of everything you see that's positive—even if it seems like there are more of them than you expected. Pay attention to how many of your perceived weaknesses come to mind, too, and then let them pass without counting them. Journal your results.

Only take Step 2 after you've completed Step 1.

Step 2. Make an appointment with someone who loves you; ask for about an hour of her time. When you're together, in a place where you won't be disturbed, ask her to tell you about the strengths she sees in you. Just listen—refrain from qualifying or discounting anything she says.

Step 3. Once she's finished telling you what she sees in you, share your list of strengths with her. What does she see that you didn't? Talk about it. Find out how she saw the strengths you've missed, and notice what you discover.

Your mission going forward is to look for those strengths in yourself that you've missed by *acting as if you have what it takes.* Try it on for size and see what happens. Supplement your practice by looking for your positive qualities every time you look in the mirror. It will help you get comfortable with looking yourself in the eyes.

Strategy #2: The Best Friend Technique

This strategy comes from my best friend, Maggie, whom I met in 1982 when we were substance abuse counselors together at NAS Chase Field. As our friendship developed over the next two years, we realized that although we spoke very positively to each other and to everyone else, we both spoke very harshly to ourselves. We each credit the other with developing this technique; odds are high that it was a true collaboration.

Here's how it works:

1. Get a pencil (not a pen) and a 3x5 card.

2. On the card, start a message to your best friend with an endearment of some kind, like "Dearest Maggie,"
3. Write a three-sentence message of love to your best friend. Tell her all the things you love about her. Be as specific and tender as possible—write from your heart.
4. Sign the card with another endearment like "With all of my love,"
5. Sign your name.
6. Now go back up to the top of the card. Erase your friend's name and write in your own.
7. Read the entire card to yourself *out loud.*
8. Carry this card with you for the next ninety days. *Whenever you start to talk harshly to yourself or berate yourself for some mistake, pull the card out and read it to yourself. See what happens.*

How did it feel to work though that exercise? If it felt wonderful, that's great. You're ready to see in yourself all those qualities that you share with your best friend. Research shows that "like attracts like," and that those people who are closest to us have beliefs, values, and opinions that are similar to ours. (Our 1st Gears match on multiple levels.)

If the exercise felt difficult, or you felt uneasy, don't worry. It may take you a little more time to see your own strengths. When I first did this exercise and read my card, I thought it sounded more like Maggie talking than me; she felt the same way about her card sounding like me. We helped each other get through this difficult period by imagining that what we'd written was coming from the other. As we practiced reading our cards to ourselves, we began hearing those powerfully positive things in the other person's voice—until we finally managed to hear them in our own.

The seeds we planted in those early days have blossomed into a friendship that has lasted over thirty years and transformed both our lives.

Taking the Next Step

Now you've explored Belief #1 and Belief #2 of Powerful Presence. You've seen the impact of believing that *you bring about what you think about,* and you know how to recognize the evidence that *you have what it takes to succeed.* At this point, you're ready for Belief #3: *Every obstacle brings a gift.* That's the topic of the next chapter.

Dance into Your Power

Chapter 13

Belief #3: Every Obstacle Brings a Gift

Obstacles are a fact of life.

Imagine what kind of journey Dorothy would have had through Oz without the obstacles she faced. Think about any book or movie you love; isn't overcoming some obstacle the whole point of the story? Overcoming obstacles is the only way we grow. You do not, however, have to suffer.

From reading the previous chapters of this book, you've seen how *you bring about what you think about* and you've discovered that you can choose your thoughts. In the last chapter you explored the idea that when you believe *you have what it takes*, you can accomplish anything.

Belief #3, believing that *every obstacle brings a gift*, is the dancer's decision.

Think about it. Have you ever heard of a dancer who didn't think she had the ability to conquer whatever obstacle in choreography she faced? Great dancers make the most difficult choreography look effortless—that's what makes them great.

The rest of us never see the months of rehearsals she's endured or the grueling hours of working tired muscles to perfect a dance whose performance takes only minutes. You only see the results: a dancer overcoming the bounds of space and gravity to capture your heart and imagination. Dancing transforms the experience of those who do it and those who witness it.

The dancer's experience teaches us that our obstacles are the catalysts for our growth and development. Although our obstacles help us grow, I'm not suggesting that we have to like them. I am suggesting that we can choose to believe that every obstacle brings us a gift, even though we may not be able to see it right away. I'm also suggesting that looking for that gift will help us reduce—and even eliminate—the suffering we might otherwise feel in the midst of our own obstacles.

Remember Charlie in the barn? Because he was focused on the gift he believed was there, he whistled while he worked. Dancers know that on the other side of an obstacle is something they want; they face their obstacles with their heads held high and their arms wide open. Like Charlie, they focus on the gift.

Remember the reticular activating system (RAS)? Your RAS filters your experience, programmed by your beliefs. When you filter for the gifts in challenging experiences, you discover things that would otherwise be invisible to you. Your RAS helps you bring about what you think about; focusing on the gift in the midst of an obstacle changes your experience of it.

Remember our Powerful Presence role models? Viktor Frankl focused on hope in the midst of despair; Helen Keller focused on ability in the midst of multiple disabilities; and Nelson Mandela focused on freedom in the midst of imprisonment.

How about you? When you look back on your life, can you see the gifts that your difficulties brought you—now that you have the distance of hindsight?

Take Action

Take a moment now to look back over the obstacles and difficulties you've faced over the last ten or twenty years. What gifts do you think those experiences have brought you? Write down your thoughts in your journal.

If you've discovered the gifts your difficulties brought you, you may be able to see that you've learned something simply by living through and getting past them. You've grown in ways that allow you to overcome future obstacles with approaches that weren't possible before your difficulties.

In case this seems a little farfetched to you right now, let me assure you that it seems that way in your 1st Gear. It's the truth for you at this moment. If you're in the midst of an obstacle right now, this belief may be a very big stretch for you. I understand. I have the benefit of hindsight to see that it took all the difficulties and challenges of my life to get me here. The Journey to Powerful Presence is built on the gifts I received from all the difficulties I faced growing up, leaving home, and then failing miserably at a lot of things for a very long time.

The perspective I got from failure and misery has helped me tremendously in the work I do now. There is no difficulty my clients face that I can't walk through with them. Overcoming my own difficulties and learning to grow through them has given me a treasure trove of distinctions, structures, and strategies that I could never have discovered any other way.

The Next Step

Now that you've discovered the secret power of hindsight, here's the next step: The secret of believing that every obstacle brings a gift is deciding that each obstacle has a gift for you without waiting for the benefit of hindsight.

The moment a difficulty or obstacle hits, decide to look for the gift. Look for it immediately—or as quickly as you can. You make the dancer's decision when you shift your thinking from disaster to opportunity.

When I mapped it out, I discovered that this belief has a three-step structure:

Step 1. Use hindsight to check your own life. Look for the gifts that your obstacles have brought you. What distinctions, structures, or strategies do you have now that you couldn't have gotten any other way? List them in your journal; becoming aware of them is your first step.

Step 2. Once you find the gifts from your past, it's easier to imagine that your current obstacles can provide you with gifts as well. Just being open to that possibility is your second step.

Step 3. As soon as you're ready, make the dancer's decision: Look for the gifts in the obstacles you currently face. Even if you can't see them right away, don't worry. The fact that you're looking for them changes your focus—and that will shape your experience in a more positive way. Taking this third step will change your life.

Let me show you what I mean. The following article first appeared in the *Discovering Your Powerful Presence Newsletter* in November of 2009. In April of 2012, it was published in my last book, *The Traveler's Pocket Guide to Powerful Presence*.

Belief #3: Every Obstacle Brings A Gift

Finding a gift in an obstacle is easier said than done, especially when you're right in the middle of the obstacle. As potent as it is, this third belief of Powerful Presence is also the trickiest to bring about.

Most people don't like to talk about their obstacles. They're so personal and individual that nobody can truly understand what you're going through when you're in the middle of it. The experience takes time to process.

The trick in handling obstacles is to look at them from a distance; when you do that, you will discover there's a pattern to experiencing them:

1. *there is an obstacle: you hit it or it hits you*
2. *there is an impact on your life that you have to work through*
3. *there is a gift for you: knowledge, experience, insight, opportunity—or something else*

Distance helped me see the gift in an obstacle that seemed insurmountable last year.

The Obstacle Hit

My home, and the land on which it stands, provides me with endless inspiration: to write, to dream, and to create. Since March 2005, it has provided a haven for my soul and a canvas for Chuck's gardening and photographic mastery. This is our home—the one we plan to live in for the rest of our days.

It is also the home of an interstate gas pipeline that diagonally bisects our backyard, travelling across I-77 from the east, headed towards the township tennis courts a few miles away to the west. The pipeline became an obstacle to the enjoyment of our haven in September 2008, when the gas company's contractor lumberjacks showed up one morning to clear the pipeline easement. They spent the day hacking the limbs off of our sixty-foot trees and cutting forty others down to stumps, leaving a forty-foot swath through our previously secluded backyard.

The Impact

When they finished, our backyard looked like it had been attacked by a giant can-opener on both ends; our once idyllic retreat was now exposed to traffic noise from the highway and bright lights from the tennis courts. And there was absolutely nothing we could do about it.

To say that we were devastated would be an understatement; we were in shock. We could not even feel the break in our hearts until weeks later, because we couldn't feel anything. We went through every one of the five stages of grief as we mourned the trees and the space like beloved family members.

The Gift

After several long months, we finally stopped looking at the "wound" in our yard. Winter passed. Spring followed. The trees emerged with crowns of green; flowers bloomed through the summer.

One late summer morning, from our kitchen window, I noticed how transcendent the light seemed as the sun rose directly over that wound in our yard. That's when we started paying attention; we discovered that the setting sun also sent light streams of red and gold through the windows in ways that had not been possible when the trees were there.

Then we started to notice the moon, visiting our yard as she rose on the horizon, fully visible in all of her phases. We started calling our wound "Moon Alley."

A year ago, the gas company's action on our property was a huge obstacle to our happiness in the home that we love. Even though I have long held — and taught — the idea that every obstacle brings a gift, this one took a while. From this distance I realize that no matter how long it takes, the gift awaits.

If there are obstacles in your life right now, know this: the gift is waiting for you, even if it takes some time to find it.

Just keep looking.

Our experience with Moon Alley created a visual reminder for me that every obstacle brings a gift. Every day I look at our garden—now full of sun-loving flowers—I remember that it was only possible once the trees were gone. My flowers remind me every day to look for the gift in whatever difficulty arises. That perspective (3rd Gear) helps me to be a resource for my clients when they face difficulties of their own.

Strategies for Practicing This Belief

Like the previous beliefs you've read about, this one will only be true for you when you try it out for yourself. Here are some strategies you can use to do that:

1. Choose your thoughts. What can you say to yourself when disaster hits? Here are some of my favorites:
   a. "There's a gift in this obstacle and I have what it takes to find it."
   b. "With all the manure around here, I know there's got to be a PONY!"
   c. "Five years from now, I'm going to be so proud of myself for overcoming this! So I'm going to start being proud of myself right now. Good job, Maia!"

2. Choose your perspective. If this looks like a disaster in your 1st Gear:
   a. Shift into neutral.
   b. Take all the time you need in neutral until you've diffused the emotion from your 1st Gear.
   c. When you're ready, shift into 3rd Gear and consider the entire situation with some distance and some logic. Just this cooling off of your emotions will help you move forward in a more resourceful way.

3. Choose your options. When a door closes, look for the open window. Use the strategies you know from your two previous beliefs:
   a. Choose optimism, like Charlie did.
   b. Use the Clock Face Technique.
   c. Use the Best Friend Technique.

Take Action

In 1st Gear, journal your thoughts about what you just read about Belief #3. What was easy for you? What was difficult? Now look back on the itinerary you created in Part Two and decide what action you want to take with this belief to move yourself closer to the destination you've chosen.

Congratulations! You've now completed Part Three. You've learned a lot about beliefs—something that required a great deal of work on your part. We're more than a third of the way into our Journey and you've done a wonderful job.

I hope you'll take a moment now to congratulate yourself on your accomplishments. At this part of the Journey, it's time to take a moment to celebrate yourself.

No journey can be taken without time for rest and relaxation, even if it's simply to gather your strength for the next part of the road. Before you read any further, close this book and do something really nice for yourself. Wait at least twenty-four hours before you start Part Four.

Celebrate!

Part Four

Three Resourceful Abilities

Dance into Your Power

Chapter 14

Developing the Three Resourceful Abilities

We've traveled some distance together already by preparing, creating an itinerary, packing our bags with the Gears, and exploring the Three Empowering Beliefs and the theory behind them.

You may remember from the Introduction that Powerful Presence is the ability to:

1. Be conscious of your actions and your impact.
2. Create spontaneous conversation with anyone, anywhere.
3. Speak, in public or in private, with confidence, flexibility, and ease.

These three behaviors are possible because of the Three Empowering Beliefs, Three Resourceful Abilities, and Three Focused Actions. You've already explored the Three Empowering Beliefs in Part Three, and you'll explore the Three Focused Actions in Part Five.

Now we're at the heart of our Journey, where we'll delve into the Three Resourceful Abilities that are the foundation of Powerful Presence:

1 Walk your talk with integrity.
2. Relate to others.
3. Dance with whatever shows up.

Before we begin our exploration of these three specific abilities, let's take a moment to explore the concept of ability in general. What does it mean to have an ability? Is an ability something you're born with—or is it something else?

If you look up the word *ability*, you'll find a variety of definitions that point you to three critical distinctions:

1. If you have an ability, it means you are able to do something or act in a certain way.
2. This ability can be the result of natural talent.
3. This ability can be the result of training—abilities can be learned.

It may seem that people with Powerful Presence must have been born with that "special something" that other people don't have. Nothing could be further from the truth. What sets these people apart is that they are conscious of their actions and their impact. You experience the energy of their presence because they have empowering beliefs and resourceful abilities, and they take focused actions.

The Three Resourceful Abilities we'll explore in this part of the book follow the perspectives of the three Gears:

- 1st Gear: The ability is "Walk your talk with integrity." You have to take the time and make the effort to take a good look at yourself; you have to decide who you are and what you want. As a result, you know yourself so well that you become comfortable in your own skin; you have confidence, flexibility, and ease in any situation.

- 2nd Gear: The ability is "Relate to others." You have to be willing to explore some things about other people that may not be true for you. Using 2nd Gear, you have to walk a few miles in other people's shoes. The more you know about other people's communication preferences, the easier it will be to listen well enough to create rapport wherever you are. As a result, you can create spontaneous conversation with anyone and speak in public with confidence, flexibility, and ease.

- 3rd Gear: The ability is "Dance with whatever shows up." You have to be willing to detach from your own 1st Gear long enough to see the bigger picture in any situation. Stepping outside of your immediate experience into 3rd Gear allows you to learn to dance, which is the antidote to getting stuck. As a result, you develop confidence, flexibility, and ease in a wider and wider range of circumstances.

As a result of developing these Three Resourceful Abilities, you'll become more conscious of your actions and your impact. When you find that your presence is not as powerful as you want it to be, you'll know exactly what to do to dance back into your own power.

Now that you've had a glimpse of the road we'll be taking, there's an important distinction to be made at this point on your Journey. Although choosing a belief is a one-time decision, developing an ability can take a lifetime. As they say, "A journey of a thousand miles begins with the first step."

The next four chapters will give you the distinctions, structures, and strategies to take your first steps.

Dance into Your Power

Chapter 15

Ability #1: Walk Your Talk with Integrity

What do you like the most about yourself?

Forty years ago, if someone had asked me that question, I would have had a difficult time coming up with an answer. It would have been much easier to tell them all the things I didn't like about myself and all the reasons why I would rather be somebody else. Although forty years ago I had a light burning inside me that other people could see, it was invisible to me.

These days, I know that I am full of Light. I know my strengths and I know my weaknesses. I've used my strengths to build the life of my dreams and I've accepted my weaknesses as part of what makes me human. I'm at peace with myself—and I'm more successful in my life today than I've ever been.

What made the difference? Once I decided that the pain of believing in my worthlessness was worse than the pain of discovering who

I might be, I had the incentive to find out. Although my Journey took years, I soon realized that the process began to speed up after a while. The more I discovered about myself, the easier the next discoveries became. The more I looked, the more I wanted to look. Once I reached the core of me, I felt as if I'd finally come home.

The outcome of taking this Journey to my core left me with the ability to:

1. identify whether what I was saying matched how I was feeling
2. access the behaviors that kept my actions congruent with my feelings
3. practice being congruent at every opportunity

In the process, I became much quicker at identifying whether I was acting congruently or not. It became exceptionally clear that being congruent increased the power of my presence—and being incongruent decreased it. Over the years, I developed the ability to *walk my talk with integrity*, and it transformed my life.

When I looked back on it, I was stunned to realize that my entire Journey was comprised of a three-step strategy:

Step 1.   Investigate.
Step 2.   Decide.
Step 3.   Act.

In order to be congruent—so we can *walk our talk with integrity*— each of us must decide what we want—in 1st Gear. Knowing that, my teachers, counselors, and role models gave me the opportunity to investigate the distinctions, structures, and strategies they shared with me. Then they asked me to make decisions about what I wanted to do, and act on them. If a decision didn't work out, they helped me use what happened as a lesson in what to do the next time. After that, my only job was to practice so I could make what I learned my own.

Remember the "take inventory" strategy in Chapter 12 (Strategy #1)? It began with an opportunity to *investigate* your awareness of your strengths and then compare them to the strengths that someone who loves you sees in you so you can *decide* whether you can believe that *you have what it takes*. Once you choose that belief, you have the opportunity to *act* using the practice of "act as if."

When you practiced the "take inventory" strategy, you experienced my three-step strategy. This ability to walk your talk with integrity is as simple as telling the truth about who you are and what you want in every moment. We'll spend the rest of this chapter exploring the strategy of:

1. Investigate,
2. decide, and
3. act

so you can discover your walk, hear your talk, and determine how closely they match. Then you can decide what you want to do about it. Once you master this strategy, it will serve you well for the rest of your life.

Step 1: Investigate

As a result of teaching this strategy in my classes and teleclasses, it's become very clear that some people are great at investigating because it's fun for them. There are others who've never considered it or who think they don't do it well. Which are you?

Before we dig a little deeper into this, take a moment to consider your own experience with investigating. Record what you find in your journal.

Take Action ————————————————————

In your journal, answer these three questions:

1. What does *investigate* mean for you?
2. What kinds of things do you already investigate?
3. How do you do it?

Congratulations! When you chose to answer those questions, you investigated something. What did you discover?

If you're good at investigating, then you're good at being curious. You're good at just poking around, looking and listening for what's there. You may even enjoy reading detective stories or watching movies and TV shows about detectives.

If you're not good at investigating yet, you can certainly learn to get better at it once you discover that investigating has a structure you can follow. The structure of investigating is this:

1. Ask a question.
2. Shift into 3rd Gear so you're as open as possible to everything around you.
3. Explore every avenue of information related to that question using your eyes, ears, and all of your senses to gather data.

That's it. The secret to your success as an investigator is simply this: *gather data.*

Being patient enough to explore every possibility without making decisions about them or acting on them prematurely is a skill you can develop.

When I first started developing this skill, I wasn't very good at it. I was much more impulsive than was useful for me. I had a hair-trigger for action that prevented me from taking the time to investigate. As you can imagine, I made decisions I regretted and took actions that were not in my best interests.

What helped me tremendously was discovering that I had a role model for investigating: Sir Arthur Conan Doyle's character Sherlock Holmes. Although there are other detectives who make great role models, Mr. Holmes was simply the ultimate for me.

I discovered Sherlock Holmes at the age of ten when my father shared the story *The Hound of the Baskervilles* with me. I'll never forget how thrilled I was to read it and how delighted I was to have this moment of peace and shared interest with my father.

It didn't take long for me to get my hands on every Sherlock Holmes story available and read them—over and over. When I was twenty-five, I purchased a two-volume set of every story, *The Annotated Sherlock Holmes*, edited by William S. Baring Gould. I still read it once a year. I've seen every movie about Holmes, starting with those 1939 black-and-white Basil Rathbone movies on TV when I was a kid, through the latest movies with Robert Downey Jr. over forty years later.

As it became clear to me on my Journey that a character I had loved since childhood was doing something I was not, I read the stories again looking for clues about his methods. My investigation proved very useful. Once I began "acting as if" I was Sherlock Holmes, my results astounded me.

Three of Sherlock Holmes's behaviors stood out for me in stark contrast to my own:

1. He was patient with his findings and took his time gathering every bit of data, no matter how obscure. Identifying his patience helped me spotlight my own impulsiveness.
2. He was methodical, starting with the data he got from his clients and investigating every element that could possibly connect to it. Identifying his methods helped me see that I had none.

3. He was logical, and never let emotion interfere with gathering data. Identifying his logical behavior helped me see how detrimental my emotion was to an investigation.

As he would say, it was "Elementary, my dear Watson."

Now that you have the structure of investigation, let's take it out for a drive. *Walking your talk with integrity* means that you have to be very clear about what's true for you—in 1st Gear. Here's where you can start to explore your desires and see if you're living in a way that's congruent with them.

— Take Action —

Find some time in your schedule for three one-hour blocks of time in the next week to ten days. Take a look at the three questions below and investigate only one of them in each of your hour-long blocks of time.

1. Who are you when nobody's looking?
2. If money were no object, what would you be doing?
3. What is the most important thing in the world to you?

During each session, record what you discover in your journal. Refrain from deciding anything about the data you collect as you record it. Take no action on your discoveries until you've completed all the work in this chapter.

Step 2: Decide

The second step in our three-step strategy for walking your talk with integrity is to decide.

The Dancers in my classes have taught me that just like with investigating, some people are great at deciding, while others just never get around to it. When you don't decide for yourself, you're often at the mercy of other people's decisions, whether they suit you or not. Those who are great at deciding are often not as skilled at investigating. You won't be surprised that the reverse is also true. How about you?

> ### ┌─ Take Action ─────────────────────────────
>
> Take just a moment before you read any further and consider your own experience with deciding. What makes it easy for you? What makes it difficult? If you're skilled at deciding, how do you do it?

You've just done some more investigating, and that will help you going forward.

You may find that you're great at deciding already. If that's the case, you may have a process that makes this easy to do. If you've discovered just the opposite, that's good news, too. What comes next is the structure of decision-making and several strategies you can use or adapt.

People who are great at decision-making have a strategy they depend on that takes their 1st Gear emotion out of the process and transforms it into 3rd Gear data. If you've ever made a decision in the midst of emotion, you know the consequences of making a snap decision you regretted later.

When I woke up to the fact that my hair-trigger emotional decision-making strategies were helping me make decisions that were at the least ineffective, and at the most harmful to me, I didn't have a plan for doing things differently. Fortunately, I had help in overcoming my decision-making challenges and my hair-trigger reactions. There were three strategies that helped me create a plan that's worked for me—and helped my clients as well:

1. **Developing criteria:** In the mid-eighties, my counselor, Mary Lou Holt, helped me see the usefulness of choosing criteria to make decisions, and the simplicity of using a decision grid. Once I mastered these two strategies, I began

making informed decisions that helped me build the life of my dreams—without the side effect of regrets.

2. **Choosing my "yeses" and "nos":** Also in the mid-eighties, in my training as a substance abuse counselor, I learned about the mathematical relationship between yes and no. Every yes costs you a no somewhere else; every no buys you a yes for something else. Each of us has 10 yeses a day to spend. After that, even if you say yes, it's really a no.

3. **Creating the 10 Commandments for my life:** Twenty-five years later, my business coach, Lenora Edwards, taught me an idea she calls "The 10 Commandments of Your Life." Although Lenora uses it to help her clients achieve amazing results in their businesses, my success with it led me to adapt it for my whole life. It's another version of choosing criteria, simply on a larger scale.

Once you learn how to use these strategies, you'll find that decision-making is a very simple and straightforward process. The only other thing you'll need is the data you've collected in the previous step.

Let's take these strategies one by one.

Strategy #1: Developing Criteria

Criteria is the plural of *criterion*. This old-fashioned word can help you achieve remarkable results when you put it into practice. A criterion is simply a standard on which a decision is based.

Even though we might not be aware of it, we all use criteria all the time—for what we want and don't want, or for what we like and don't like.

For example, what's your favorite kind of food? Your favorite kind of food is a standard upon which you can base your decision about eating at someone's house, cooking for yourself, or eating out at a restaurant. Say your favorite food is Italian, and someone asks you out for sushi. You have a standard for what you like the best, and it's not sushi. If your criterion for what you won't eat includes raw fish, then it's very easy to say "No, thanks!" because you're very clear that you won't like it, even if you've never tried it. If, however, you've never heard of sushi and you have a criterion for adventurous eating that doesn't preclude raw fish, you might say "Sure!" Sounds very simple, doesn't it?

Food is a simple example; let's make it a little more complicated and take a look at the criteria we use for travel. Where is someplace you'd really enjoy going? If, like me, you chose The Republic of Ireland, odds are high that your criteria include a number of things like:

- the climate: temperate, with warm summers and mild winters
- the language you'd want to hear: lilted English and Gaelic
- the food you'd be eating: things you've probably eaten before with some engaging new possibilities

If, however, you chose someplace like Goa, India, your criteria are likely very different:

- the climate: tropical monsoon climate; hot and humid most of the year
- the language you'd want to hear: Konkani, an Indo-European language
- the food you'd be eating: rice with fish curry; lots of fish in elaborate recipes; dishes with coconut, coconut oil, chili peppers, spices, and vinegar; pork dishes (vindaloo); khatkhate (an exotic vegetable stew); and sannas (spongy, steamed, savory rice cakes)

In my leadership training, my Norwegian friend, Inger, told me about the winter vacations she took in Goa every year with her Indian husband. Inger loved Goa so much that her descriptions of it made for some wonderful daydreams of the trip Chuck and I would take to visit her and her husband there—until I realized that it didn't meet my criteria for climate. As much as our conversations about it made me long to go there, my requirements for temperature made it impossible for me to consider it any further. It was a very easy decision.

It's easy to see how criteria help you make simple decisions about food and travel. How about the deeper questions of who you want to be and what you want to do? Even though those questions are more profound, criteria works just as effectively to help you make decisions about your life. *We'll come back to that in a moment.*

So criteria are the standards you have for what you want and don't want, and what you like and don't like. How do you find out what they are? You investigate!

> ### Take Action
>
> In your journal, make a list of 10 Things That You Want and 10 Things That You Don't Want. Make another list of 10 Things That You Like and 10 Things That You Don't Like. What did you discover? These are some of your standards—your criteria—and they're all in 1st Gear.

Decision Grids

When I was first learning to decide, it was challenging for me to weigh all the factors involved because everything was so emotional for me. Hair-trigger decisions that I often regretted were my norm. Then I learned about decision grids.

A decision grid allows you to lay out all the information you have as a result of your investigation so you can make an informed decision in 3rd Gear. If you've ever heard of a cost benefit analysis, this grid may look familiar.

The process works like this:

1. Get a blank piece of notebook or copy paper.

2. Write the issue you need to make a decision about across the top of the page.
3. Create two columns by drawing a vertical line down the middle of the paper.
4. At the top of the left column, write "Do."
5. At the top of the right column, write "Not Do."
6. Right under the word *Do*, write "What will it cost me to do this?"
7. Right under the words *Not Do*, write "What will it cost me to not do this?"
8. Now make a horizontal line across the middle of the page, about halfway down.
9. Just under that line, in the left column, write "What are the benefits of doing this?"
10. Just under that line, in the right column, write "What are the benefits of not doing this?"
11. Now you've got four spaces to fill in. Take some quiet time where you'll be undisturbed and fill in everything you can—in 1st Gear. Once you've made a first pass at it, it can help to confer with someone you trust to be sure you've filled in everything possible in all four spaces.

Once you have it all filled in, you can compare the costs and benefits of doing something or not doing it. In every case, your decision will be obvious, as well as in 3rd Gear.

Try this out for yourself and see how it works.

┌─ Take Action ─

Take a blank piece of notebook or copy paper and create a decision grid for yourself.

If you're using the electronic journal from my website, you'll find a decision grid has already been created for you. If you're using your own journal, you'll find a decision grid here: *www. maiabeatty.com/PDFs/mydecisiongrid.pdf*

> If you have a decision to make that you've been unable to work through, take the time to work it through now using your decision grid.
>
> Document your results in your journal.

Strategy #2: Choose Your Yeses and Nos

As a substance abuse counselor in the eighties, I learned that yes and no have a mathematical relationship. Why hadn't anyone ever told me that before?

Growing up, I learned that no was not a word I was allowed to say. The answer to every request of the grown-ups in my life was "Yes," which was to be said as pleasantly as possible. I can remember my sister Deirdre saying "NO!" with great enthusiasm as a two-year-old. Before she was three, she had been trained to remove that word from her vocabulary.

As I was developing my ability to say no, it became very clear to me why many people, and especially women, have such a hard time saying no. We've been socialized out of it—just like those baby elephants.

One of my favorite quotes from that time in my life is this one: "If you can't say no, then yes is just a noise you're making with your mouth. It doesn't mean a thing. There is no true yes without the alternative of an emphatic no." Although I can't remember which of my instructors at the Navy's Counseling and Assistance Center Training School said it, I've never forgotten that quote.

As exciting as that quote was for me, the roots of my early training were very deep; it took me years to be able to say no without feeling very guilty. It's clear to me now that my guilt was simply the residue of my training as I struggled to develop this ability. Once I got conscious of what it was costing me to say yes when I meant no, my experience proved to me the usefulness of the idea that "there is no true yes without an emphatic no." As a result, I decided to reclaim my nos; I even learned to say them as a complete sentence.

"No."

At that point, my guilt disappeared.

If you're still feeling guilty about saying no, it's very difficult to walk your talk with integrity. When inside you the answer to a request is no, yet you feel you have to say yes to the other person, you've just been untrue to yourself. Over time, the incongruity between how you feel on the inside and what you present to the world prevents you from knowing what you really want and who you really are. This makes it difficult to distinguish your personal criteria for decision-making.

The way out of this guilt is to investigate the mathematical relationship between your yeses and your nos. When you take the time to do that, you'll discover how many of the yeses you say to other people result in the nos you say to yourself. When you remember that the hallmark of Powerful Presence is being conscious of your actions and your impact, you'll find that investigating the relationship between your yeses and nos increases the power of your presence.

Don't take my word for this. Try it out for yourself.

Take Action

Start with a clean page in your journal and divide it in half with a vertical line down the middle. At the top of the left-hand side of the page, write "Things I Say Yes To." At the top of the right hand side of the page, write "Things I Say No To." Start listing your yeses and nos until you fill the page. It doesn't matter how long it takes. What matters is that you list as many as you can think of until you fill the page. Once the page is full, take a look at what you've written and see what pattern emerges. On the next page in your journal, record your findings. What did you discover? Record that, too.

A Powerful Structure: 10 Yeses a Day

In my training as a substance abuse counselor, I learned that one of the challenges many people face is feeling that they must say yes to everyone but themselves. Doing this completely depletes your physical, mental, emotional and spiritual resources. If saying yes is a reflex for you, you may have discovered in the Take Action exercise above that you're saying yes more than 10 times a day, and you're keeping very few of those yeses for yourself.

If we've been trained as children to deny ourselves in favor of pleasing everyone else, this is a very difficult pattern to break. Like baby elephants, all of our training points to pleasing others and ignoring ourselves. For some of us, saying yes to others feels like a requirement for survival.

As a counselor, I learned a very powerful strategy that helped me a great deal; it often astonishes my clients when I share it with them. It goes like this: You have 10 yeses a day to spend, and every day you start out with 10 fresh yeses. You always have a choice about your yeses. You can spend them all on other people or you can spend some on yourself. You can try to hoard them and say no to everything. No matter what you do with them, you still only have 10 yeses each day. People with Powerful Presence spend all of their yeses every day on the things that are most important to them; they make sure that they spend two or three of those daily yeses on themselves.

When you think about it, it's just plain math. Figure out how many hours you're awake in a typical a day—it's about sixteen if you want to get a good night's sleep. It's easy to see that with only sixteen hours to do it in, you can say yes effectively only 10 times.

Think about the number of yeses you have to say every day just to keep your life going. For most people, their #1 Yes goes to their job or to their family. Then #2 goes to the other one—job and family are

#1 and #2 for most people. Sometimes you can use up all 10 of your yeses on just your job and your family!

If you're getting a college degree, that's a yes. If you have a second job, that's another yes. If you have aging parents you're caring for as you're raising your children, that's another yes.

When you do the math, you'll find that you only have a certain number of hours in a day. The limits on your time require that you have an easy way to decide how you spent those hours; that's why you need to have *criteria*. When you know what you want and what you don't want, it's much easier to decide where to spend your yeses. Once they're spent, everything else is a no.

If you're wondering how that could be so, consider your own experience. Have you ever had to readjust your schedule because you agreed to do something that you discovered at the eleventh hour you couldn't pull off? That's just one example of spending a yes that was really a no.

When you're having trouble deciding whether or not to say yes to something, you can use a decision grid to map it out in 3rd Gear for yourself.

The most important quality of Powerful Presence is the ability to be conscious of your actions and your impact. When you get conscious of the way you're spending your yeses and nos, you will transform your life.

Strategy #3: Create the 10 Commandments for Your Life

My coach Lenora Edwards taught me many things that have transformed my business and the way I think. The success I've had in the past five years is due in part to her helping me focus my energy and attention. Early in our work together, she helped me hone my strategy for yeses and nos into a fine art.

Lenora taught me that creating 10 Commandments for myself would laser my focus so clearly that my 10 yeses a day would become "Heck, Yes!" Everything else becomes "Heck, No!" She was right. Once I identified my 10 Commandments, I was exceptionally clear about my mission in life and how I wanted to live it. There wasn't a single doubt left in my mind. Since then, my results have been nothing short of remarkable; I've accomplished more in the last three years than I have in the last ten.

Below is my statement of 10 Commandments that Lenora helped me create in 2009:

My 10 Commandments

In order to be the most successful in helping people discover and develop their Powerful Presence, I, Maia Beatty, must:

1. Do work that has heart and meaning.
2. Work with people who regularly invest in their professional development.
3. Work with people who are willing to do deep work.
4. Work with people who have the financial resources to pay my fee up front and require no more than two meetings with me to decide to work with me.
5. Work with the decision-maker.
6. Regularly request recommendations and referrals.
7. Be grounded with daily physical exercise and meditation so I can do remarkable, referable work.
8. Have enough down time in nature and with Chuck to stay creative.
9. Have regular writing time each week.
10. Invest in my own professional and personal development.

These personal commandments were easy to come up with after I created a list like the one you saw in an earlier Take Action exercise: I listed what I wanted and didn't want and what I liked and didn't like. Once I looked at what I'd written, my 10 Commandments fell right into my lap.

Once again, this only makes sense when you try it yourself.

Take Action

Go back to page 164 and the page you used in your journal for the Take Action exercise in which you listed the Things You Like and Don't Like and the Things You Want and Don't Want. Use them to create your own 10 Commandments. What did you discover? Are your yeses congruent with your 10 Commandments? If they are—that's great. If they're not, don't worry. Now you have the perfect evidence you need to take action.

Now that you've explored what it takes to investigate and what it takes to decide, all that's left to do is act.

Step 3: Act

Everything you've just discovered about yourself is irrelevant— unless you make it real with action.

When you investigate, it's important that you simply gather the data without deciding or acting until you've gathered enough of it to be thorough. In order to decide, you have to be clear about which of the available actions are most congruent with your personal desires and outcomes. Once you've decided what you want to do, you have to act.

A decision without action neutralizes the decision.

Walking your talk with integrity is simple when your inside thoughts match your outside behavior. Developing and refining this ability is a mission that continues throughout your lifetime. The more you do it, the easier it gets.

Like every journey, this one begins with the first step. This chapter gives you the first steps toward increasing your ability to walk your talk with integrity. When you take action with what you've learned, you can hone this ability into an instinct.

Now that you've explored Ability #1, Ability #2 awaits you in the next chapter: *Relate to others*.

Chapter 16

Ability #2: Relate to Others

To paraphrase John Donne, no one is an island.

We live our lives in the midst of others, so our ability to relate to them affects our presence. If we want it to be powerful, we have to find a way to relate to most people in a positive way.

My early experiences in life fueled a desire in me to do just that; they led me to the strategies in this chapter.

In the midst of my family, I felt like I didn't fit in. From third grade to seventh grade, I was in a new school every year. As the new kid at the start of each year, I didn't fit in at school either. As a result, I didn't have a clue how to *relate to others*. In my home I was taught to obey, which I wasn't very good at; I was usually in trouble there and at school for doing things my own way. I typically had more fun being alone with a book than I had being with most people I knew.

Then I got to high school and something changed. It may have been that everyone else was new just like I was; whatever it was, I lost the stigma of being "the new kid." The pure joy of connecting to others who were like me—and who liked me—is something I've never forgotten. It proved to me that there were people on the planet who enjoyed my company and who liked me just as I was.

For years after I ran away from home, I kept looking for more of those kinds of people. I knew that life would be great when I found them—just like in high school. As I traveled around the country in the Navy in my twenties, I discovered that finding people who liked me was hit-or-miss. Sometimes I found them, sometimes I didn't; sometimes they liked me, and then for reasons I couldn't fathom, they stopped liking me.

It took me a long time to figure out that my behavior had an impact on my relationships with other people. Although anyone who knows me now might find it surprising that I had no idea of my impact, it's true.

At this distance, it's clear that my focus was on getting other people to like me, and that I missed the strategy of liking myself first. I spent a lot of time focused on other people, paying attention to the way they did things so I could "fit" in their company. Although this was an indirect strategy that took a long while to pay off, my early single-minded focus on the ways others acted taught me a great deal that later helped me develop a Powerful Presence.

In the meantime, three experiences led me to major communication breakthroughs that created a strong desire to increase my skill:

- Part of the curriculum in the Navy's Counseling and Assistance Center (CAAC) Training School was being in group therapy. Every weekday, for the twelve-week duration of the training, we had group sessions that put the spotlight on how we interacted with other people. In order to be successful as a substance abuse counselor, you had to be rigorous about self-awareness—*you had to be conscious of your actions and your impact*. This group therapy was such an intrinsic part of our training that failing it would result in being dropped from the school no matter how successful you were at everything else. It was so rigorous that we lost half of our class before we graduated. Through this experience, I discovered that I had become very astute at reading other people; my challenge was to become equally astute at self-awareness. Although my grades were consistently high, I couldn't see how skilled I was with my clients. I didn't push back against our group leader if I thought she was unfair or misinformed about something in our group sessions. In my last week of school, I was on notice that this was the critical factor that would affect my ability to graduate. In our final group session, the day before we graduated, I finally claimed myself and my impact on the group in defiance of something this group leader said about my skill as a counselor. Acting on that shift in my awareness allowed me to graduate.

- While I was stationed at the CAAC in Jacksonville in 1984, I had the opportunity to attend a training course in Neurolinguistic Programming (NLP) at one of the local colleges. The course was aimed at therapists and counselors who wanted to be more effective at communicating with their patients and their clients. One of the most magical concepts I learned in that course was rapport; it took me right back to my experience in high school. I learned that I could create *rapport* with anyone by identifying, and then matching, their communication style.

- When I was pursuing my BA in the mid-eighties, I met Dr. John Wilson, the chair of the communication department. I took every class he offered for the two years I was there. He became my role model for exquisite communication in the midst of difficult circumstances. The secret to his exquisite communication was his exceptional skill at listening. He was so good at transferring his knowledge and skill to us that I became a better listener simply because I was his student. Several of the strategies I use today are modeled from things I learned in his classes.

That's my 1st Gear on developing communication skills. I've spent more than half my lifetime developing and refining my ability to relate to others. Even though it's been one of the most amazing adventures of my life, there is still so much more to learn as I develop this ability with new distinctions, structures, and strategies.

Now how about you? You've got a 1st Gear, too. Exploring your beliefs, values, opinions, and experiences in communication will help you get conscious of your actions and your impact—and increase your ability to relate to others.

Take Action

Before you read any further, consider your communication strengths by listing in your journal all the things you do well as a communicator. What did you discover? What trends and patterns did you find?

Everyone has a starting point when it comes to relating to others. As I discovered in high school, there are people with whom you naturally communicate well and situations in which your natural communication style shines. When you become aware of your communication strengths, you can build on and expand them.

If you're wondering how to start identifying your communication strengths, think about the things you do well in conversations with other people. These behaviors and skills might come easy to you, so you may have the inclination to discount them as strengths. If you find it difficult to identify your strengths, ask someone with whom you enjoy talking what it is about you that makes being in conversation with you so enjoyable. As you did in the practice in Chapter 12, when you asked someone who loves you what they see in you, just listen to what this person tells you and write those qualities down as your communication strengths.

Here are three examples of the power of discovering your communication strengths:

1. Discovering your communication strengths is the foundation of my *PowerSpeak!* class. Since 1999, thousands of my clients have come to class focusing on their speaking challenges. Focusing on their *challenges* helps keep them stuck and prevents them from being the excellent speakers they were born to be. One of our first exercises allows them to identify their speaking *strengths*. When it comes time to speak in the second half of the class, every one of them has learned to play to their strengths. Each of them has different strengths, yet all of them have a powerful speaking experience. For many of them, it's the first time in their lives they've felt powerful speaking in public.

2. In my Communication Strategies for Success classes, we start by identifying your communication strengths for the same reason: Playing to your strengths makes you a better communicator because it gives you a foundation for addressing your challenges. As you'll find in this chapter, knowing your strengths allows you to play to them as well as adapt them in your conversations so you can create rapport.

3. When I work with my coaching clients, one of the first things we do is identify their strengths. One hundred percent of them have learned how to open up new avenues of success once they know how to identify and access their strengths.

Your Communication Challenges

Once you become aware of your strengths, you have a starting point for this portion of your Journey. Next, it's important to become aware of your communication challenges so you can use your strengths—and the distinctions, structures, and strategies you'll discover here—to address them.

Take Action

On a separate page in your journal, list your communication challenges. What are the behaviors of other people that drive you crazy? What are the interpersonal situations that you find

---

difficult? What gets in the way for you when you're having trouble relating to someone? Look for patterns and trends.

Now that you've done some investigating and gathered some data, we'll connect that data with my Three Communication Breakthrough Strategies. The work of this chapter is to explore them for yourself so you can see how they work for you.

Those strategies are:

1. Focus your Attention.
2. Match the other person's communication style.
3. Address any listening barriers.

Strategy #1: Focus Your Attention

When you see the word attention, what do you think of? When I ask that question to my clients or in my classes, most people say "being aware of" or "concentrating."

How do you know you're paying attention to something? Most people tell me that they know they're paying attention to something when all of their awareness is concentrated on that one thing.

Here are three examples of this:

1. When you are so focused on doing something you love that time and space melt away. Mihaly Csikszentmihalyi calls this state Flow, and describes it as the "psychology of optimal experience." (*This flow occurs when you are alone or when all the people you're with are focused on the same task in the same way.*)
2. When you're so aware of another person that you can't feel your body or hear your own thoughts—it seems as if she is the only person in the room.

3. When you're aware of everything around you without specifically thinking about it, it makes driving, playing a sport, or dancing in a crowded club feel like instinct.

Do these examples seem familiar? How about the following examples:

- When you were little, you might have heard your parents or teachers say, "Pay attention!" How did they know you weren't?
- If you're in a relationship, you may hear from your partner, "A penny for your thoughts." How do they know you're thinking?
- Somebody walks into a crowded room and your head almost snaps to look at them. You can't focus on anything but them. How do they do that?

These examples of differently focused attention may be familiar to you, although you might not have given them a second thought. When you want to increase your Powerful Presence in the way you *relate to others*, becoming conscious of your attention is the very first place to begin.

Now that you know how important it is to consciously focus your attention, I'm going to use a capital A to indicate its significance. Getting conscious of how you're focusing your Attention is a huge part of developing your Powerful Presence.

Let's start with the basics. Over the years of experimenting with Attention, I've learned that Attention has an energy you can feel. Until you get conscious of this energy, it may escape your notice. There are three places you can focus your Attention, and each of them *feels* different. Other people can sense this difference in energy, too.

Let's start with the three places you can focus your Attention so you can check this out for yourself.

1. **Attention on you**
   a. *How you can tell:* When you focus your Attention on yourself, you can feel your body and hear your own thoughts. You have "gone inside yourself" and your Attention is internally focused.
   b. *What it's good for:* This is a great way to daydream, plan, practice playing an instrument, choreograph a dance, write, create, or process your feelings. You can even rehearse behaviors or scenarios for later use. This is what creates the "flow."
   c. *Important to note:* As great as it is for flow, this is the worst place to focus your Attention if you want to talk to someone else. Not only is it impossible to hear anything anyone else is saying with your Attention focused on yourself, you can't even share your own thoughts effectively. When you're speaking in public, focusing your Attention on yourself includes worrying about the PowerPoint or whether you left out an important point you wanted to make. When you do that, you've lost your connection with the audience and given them every reason to ignore you. Focusing your Attention on yourself when you're speaking in public creates stage fright.

2. **Attention on the other person**
   a. *How you can tell:* When you focus your Attention on another person, you're so focused on her that you can't feel your body or hear your own thoughts. This doesn't mean you can't speak! Have you ever felt so connected to another person that you said things you didn't know you were going to say? You weren't thinking of what you'd say, you were just speaking. This is a common occurrence when you have your Attention on the other person and she has hers on you.
   b. *What it's good for:* Engaging in a conversation in which communication is open and free-flowing. Communication flows between people who have focused their Attention on each other.

c. *Important to note:* This is the only way to create rapport. This works for speaking in public as well; great speakers focus their Attention on their audiences—and magic happens.

3. **Attention on everything around you:**
   a. How you can tell: Focusing your Attention on everything requires that you maintain your awareness of everything around you instead of focusing on just one thing.
   b. What it's good for: This is the secret of great drivers, anyone who plays sports well, dancers, moms, firefighters, EMT and ER personnel, divers, successful holiday shoppers at the mall, soldiers, sailors, and anyone who is successful in the midst of action.
   c. Important to note: Focusing your Attention this way allows you to respond instinctively without having to think through your choices. It provides your RAS with the widest possible filter so that whatever sensory information you need will be available to you. You've probably seen great comedians use it when they incorporate something that happens with the audience or in the room into their routine; it looks effortless. Keeping their Attention on everything is their secret. Great speakers use it to create their magic, too.

Now that you know about the three places you can focus your Attention, your mission is to do some investigating and see for yourself.

— **Take Action** —

Over the next several days, pay attention to where you're focusing your Attention. What results are you getting? Where do you naturally place your Attention? What happens when you shift it? Record your impressions in your journal; look for patterns and trends.

Strategy #2: Matching Anyone's Communication Style

Now that you know how to focus your Attention on others, you may find that you're picking up lots of clues about behavior that you never noticed before. This is very useful when you want to match the communication style of someone you're just meeting or don't know well.

Now why would you want to do that? The secret to being able to successfully *relate to others* is the ability to create rapport with anyone you meet so you can easily start a conversation with anyone, anywhere. That ability will transform your experience in business and in social situations.

When you want to increase your ability to relate to others, it's very useful to be conscious of your actions and your impact. Although there are many things you can learn about how to communicate exquisitely, it would take a whole book to begin to address them. The distinctions, structures, and strategies in this chapter will give you a great start.

You won't be surprised that there is a three-step structure for matching anyone's communication style:

Step 1. Understand the nature of rapport.
Step 2. Identify your own communication style.
Step 3. Pay attention to the differences and similarities between your style and the other person's style so you can easily match theirs—and create rapport.

Step 1: Understand the Nature of Rapport

What does the word *rapport* mean to you?

When I ask my clients and audiences what the word *rapport* means to them, they often say "trust." They also say "connection, harmony, and ease of conversation." All of those descriptions are accurate.

Rapport can be instant; when you meet someone you like right away, it's because you're naturally *in rapport* with them. When you meet someone you instantly dislike, natural rapport is missing, and you are *out of rapport*.

When you have Powerful Presence, you can create rapport when it doesn't exist by matching the communication style of anyone you meet. It simply requires that you pay attention to them and know how to match their style. Creating rapport becomes very simple once you understand that it has a structure:

> *The structure of rapport:*
> *You're like me + You like me = I like you*

If you and the other person have the same communication style, you naturally like each other. What's not to like about someone who's like you?

The reverse is also true: You naturally like someone who's like you because you have the same communication style. That's why knowing about style differences will help you create rapport with someone with whom communicating would otherwise seem difficult. Creating rapport requires that you pay attention, get in 2nd Gear, and be curious.

Paying attention makes it easy for you to identify the other person's communication style. Match their style to create rapport, and watch your conversation flow.

Step 2: Identify Your Own Communication Style

There are at least five basic communication style preferences you can identify in yourself and in other people. For the purpose of your Journey, you just need to get started with the basics.

If relating to other people was like learning to play the piano, you'd begin your journey to proficiency with finger exercises, wouldn't you? Since the first two communication style preferences are the easiest to identify, like finger exercises, they give you the best place to begin. Once you get skilled at identifying them, you'll notice that your ability to *relate to others* has increased significantly.

The *speed* at which a person communicates and the process with which they do it are the two communication style preferences that are the easiest to identify in yourself and in others. We'll explore them one at a time.

Speed

Your speed is the rate at which you communicate. It has nothing to do with intelligence, it simply relates to speed. When measured on a continuum, speed ranges from *quick* to *careful*.

How about you? Which one do you think best describes you? Are you quick—or more careful?

When I ask this question in my classes, I ask it this way: "Who's quick?" The quick ones have their hands in the air before I finish that two-word question. The rest of the class is looking at me as if to say, "I could be quick—if you would just finish the sentence. Quick about what?"

What makes this such a useful distinction is that the quick ones are quick with just about everything and the careful ones are careful with just about everything. Although we all have a range of speed in our style, we are typically either mostly quick or mostly careful. When we meet another person with the same speed, it's easy to create rapport because we're alike in our speed preference. Don't take my word for this, though. Check it out for yourself.

Take Action

Think about the speed preference of the people you like the most. Does their speed match yours? Now think about the speed preference of the people who are the most challenging for you. Are they more quick than you—or more careful? What did you discover? Record your findings in your journal.

Process

Now let's explore the second communication style preference: process. Your process is the way you prefer to interact with others. Like speed, it can be measured on a continuum with *task-focused* on one end and *relationship-focused* on the other end. Although we all have a range in our behaviors depending on the situation, we still have a preference for one or the other.

When I ask this question in class, I ask it in terms of scenarios. Think about your preferences when you go to work. Which is more true for you:

1. You're already thinking about work when you get to the front door of your workplace. You head directly to your desk, focused on the tasks you have to accomplish today. You feel moderate-to-very irritated when a co-worker tries to engage you in a conversation about your weekend before you get to your desk. You have work to do and you want to get to it. You know that your success in this organization is largely due to your technical skill; getting right to work is just one of the ways you harness that skill. You're focused on the tasks and are less personal at work. You place a high value on people who are skilled at their tasks.
2. You're thinking about the people with whom you work when you get to the front door of your workplace. You make it a point to acknowledge everyone you meet on your way to your desk, and you ask several of them a few quick questions about their weekend along the way. You feel moderate-to-very irritated when a co-worker accuses you of being lazy or unprofessional because you are engaged in personal conversations with others on your way to your desk. You know that your success in this organization is largely due to the relationships you've built, and

greeting people is just one of the ways you nourish those relationships. You're focused on the relationships and are more personal at work. You place a high value on people who get their tasks done through their relationships across the organization.

Most people have a range of behaviors that lie between those two extremes. People with Powerful Presence have learned to access both of those behaviors even though it takes more energy to access the process that is not their natural preference. Which of those process preferences is yours?

Take Action

Think about the process preference of the people you like the most. Does their process—task-focused or relationship-focused—match yours?

Now think about the process preferences of the people who are the most challenging for you. Are they more task-focused than you are—or more relationship-focused than you are?

What did you discover? Record your findings in your journal.

Step 3: Pay Attention So You Can Create Rapport

The simplest way to create rapport with anyone, anywhere, is to pay attention to them—so you can identify their speed and process and then match them.

When you investigated the speed and process preferences of the people you like the most, what did you discover? Did they match you in either one or both preferences? And how about those people you find challenging—was the opposite true?

Here's where you can use several of the distinctions, structures, and strategies you've learned on your Journey to increase your ability to *relate to others*:

1. With your Attention on yourself, get in 1st Gear and identify your speed and process. Identify your opposite: the speed and process that pose the most difficulty for you.
2. Give yourself every opportunity to match the speed and process that are most difficult for you. Give yourself time to play with this before you use it with real people. Practice matching the characters in TV shows or movies that represent your opposites. Have some fun increasing and decreasing your speed and changing up your process.
3. When you feel confident in your ability to pay attention to someone you don't like, use what you've learned to match their speed and process. Every time you interact with them, match them. You will find that over time it's much easier to find something about them you like. When you're just like them — in your speed and process — and you like them, you'll have successfully created rapport and increased the flow of your communication.

Now that you've explored the first two strategies of this ability, you're ready for the third and final one.

Strategy #3: Address Any Listening Barriers

Have you ever found that you just can't listen even when it's really important that you do?

In the last thirty years of exploring all the facets of interpersonal communication, I've discovered that it really isn't your fault. In 1992, Chuck and I made a very important medical discovery: The reason that people can't listen, even when it's really important, is because they have become prey to the most insidious listening barrier on the planet, the BEPPUMOID (bep-uh-moid).

You may never have heard of this creature before. That's why learning about it is such an important part of your Journey to Powerful Presence. Incidentally, like all medical discoveries, those who discover something often get to name it. Chuck gave it a form and I gave it a name. After all these years, it's becoming more accepted in the medical community—you can even Google it.

What Is a BEPPUMOID, and How Did We Discover It?

This is a picture of a real BEPPUMOID, magnified 100 times. Its medical name is *Listenus-not-atallus*. As tiny as a baby's fingernail, it crawls into your ear and prevents you from hearing anything anyone has to say. You can actually have a BEPPUMOID infestation—multiple creatures in one or both ears.

How can you tell if you've been infested?

Because these creatures are so tiny, you can only detect an infestation by recognizing the symptoms when someone else is talking to you.

Check this list to see if you've ever had BEPPUMOIDs in your ears. You have if you were:

- Bored
- Emotional
- Physically tired
- Preoccupied
- Uninterested
- Mentally tired
- Organizing your thoughts for a reply
- Interrupting
- Distracted

Take Action

List the symptoms of a BEPPUMOID infestation in your journal and check all those you commonly experience.

What did you discover? How many symptoms did you find in your listening behaviors?

Most of the Dancers in my Journey to Powerful Presence classes tell me that their symptoms vary depending on the situation. These days, the top three symptoms for almost everyone are:

1. Emotional
2. Physically tired
3. Mentally tired

There's something else worth pointing out about the symptoms of a BEPPUMOID infestation: *All of these symptoms occur in 1st Gear, with your Attention on yourself.* So each symptom is the truth for you, and your Attention on yourself prevents you from getting any input from anyone else.

Take Action

Let's stop here for a moment so you can take in all of your surroundings. We've been using the three Gears throughout our Journey—and now you've discovered the power of your *Attention*.

Can you see the connection between those two and listening? Does it make sense that a BEPPUMOID infestation makes it harder for you to match the speed and process of those whose speed and process are different from yours?

Making the connection between the three *Gears*, your *Attention*, matching *speed* and *process*, and *listening* is one of the ways you can increase your Powerful Presence because you're getting even more conscious of your actions and your impact. Think about the way these distinctions, structures, and strategies can affect your current relationships. Record your thoughts in your journal.

Where Did It Come From?

The BEPPUMOID has been a big hit with my audiences and clients since I created it in 1992. It's helped many thousands of people become better listeners. Now, for the first time, I want to share its origins with you.

In the midst of preparing a presentation on effective listening for a client in Corpus Christi, Texas, in 1992, I came across Madelyn Burley-Allen's excellent book, *Listening: The Forgotten Skill*. Ms. Burley-Allen used a number of distinctions I had learned in my NLP training and I thoroughly enjoyed reading her book. The term *listening barriers* is hers.

After reframing what I'd read and adapting her language to come up with my own words to describe the barriers she illustrated, I arranged the words in an order that I thought would help me remember them easily. In the process, I used the first letters of each word to arrive at the word I created, BEPPUMOID. In the process of playing with the words, it became clear to me that each description of a listening barrier would now become a symptom of a BEPPUMOID infestation. It was exciting to have a creature and to have a fun way to remember those listening barriers.

A creature, and symptoms, reminded me of something else I enjoyed immensely. Have you seen the movie *Star Trek II: The Wrath of Khan*? In that movie, Chekov and another Enterprise crew member are captured by Khan and forced to have "mind-controlling eels" dropped into their ears. The purpose of those eels was to prevent them from listening to their own thoughts or the commands of their captain; they would now be terrorists for Khan and help him destroy the *Enterprise*.

As I thought about Madelyn's listening barriers, it struck me that they were every bit as deadly to relationships as those eels were to the crew of the *Enterprise*.

That's when I knew that the BEPPUMOID was a first cousin of those eels. It gave me the perfect metaphor for getting the word out about the insidious nature of listening barriers. For over twenty years, the BEPPUMOID has been helping me spread the word about them in a tangible way.

The Effects of an Infestation

Here's why knowing about the BEPPUMOID is so important: When someone tells you something while you've got an infestation, they think you've heard them. Unfortunately, you haven't—you've only wasted their time and yours. What's worse is that they think you've received the message they delivered.

What do you think this costs relationships and organizations? How much critical information gets left by the wayside because of BEPPUMOIDs? How much unnecessary conflict arises because of the differences between your 1st Gear (you never heard it) and theirs (they know they told you)?

Now that you know the symptoms and effects of a BEPPUMOID infestation, it's important to know the antidotes.

The Antidote When You Have a BEPPUMOID

The moment you realize you have any of the symptoms of an infestation, it's important that you let the other person know about it. You can tell her you're coming down with something. (Saying the word infestation is always a choice.)

Tell her you just need to take a moment before you can listen to her. Then promise to get right back to her because you really want to hear what she has to say. Now take care of yourself right away so you can get back to her as quickly as possible. Do whatever you need to do to clear your head and take care of your symptoms so you can get in 2nd Gear, ready to listen, with your Attention on her.

The Antidote When Someone Else Has a BEPPUMOID

When you notice that the person with whom you wish to speak is exhibiting any of the symptoms of a BEPPUMOID infestation, stop yourself before telling her anything. Ask her, "Is this a good time to catch you?" That might be enough for her to be able to give you her Attention. If it isn't, ask her if you can come back later. Decide together when "later" will be and be sure to go back. When you get there, ask again, "Is this a good time to catch you?" Your Attention on her and your care for her well-being is often the trigger for her to give you her full Attention so you can get your message across.

Both of these antidotes are much easier to use when you already have rapport with this person and she trusts you.

That's why it's so important to practice putting your Attention on others and to find a way to match their speed and process so you can create rapport with them. When it comes right down to it, effective listening requires your Attention and rapport. Imagine what will happen in all of your relationships when you master these distinctions, structures, and strategies!

Take Action

Pick someone in your personal or professional life with whom you want relate more effectively. Use everything you've learned in this chapter to improve the communication between the two of you. Record your findings in your journal.

At this point in your Journey, you've explored the first two of the Three Resourceful Abilities—you've discovered how to begin to walk your talk with integrity and relate to others.

Ability #3 awaits you in the next chapter: *Dance with whatever shows up.*

Chapter 17

Ability #3: Dance with Whatever Shows Up

Before I was a dancer, I was a runner—and a fighter.

The strategy of *dancing with whatever shows up* grew out of many years of trial and error. It took me until I was in my fifties to learn that I could handle anything that showed up in my life when I just danced with it. Not only does dancing with my circumstances surpass both of my other strategies of flight and fight, it's the strategy that many of my clients tell me they use the most.

Although the road to dancing was long, it was also exceptionally illuminating.

My Journey to Dancing

Running away was my first strategy when faced with circumstances I couldn't handle. We moved a lot when I was growing up, so I learned that no matter how bad things got with a teacher or my classmates, I'd be in a new school the following year. I learned early that nothing was too big to run from. In my twenties, I heard a name for it: *the geographical cure.*

Running away kept me from getting stuck in difficult circumstances because it kept me moving. Unfortunately, running never prevented those circumstances from finding me again. The things I wouldn't handle just followed me. Then I learned about fighting.

In 1977, my first therapist, Gwen Nichols, got me started. She uncovered the deep-seated anger I was carrying around when she gave me a little exercise to do early in our therapeutic relationship. In a discussion in which she pointed out that she thought I was a very angry girl, and I denied it, she invited me to use my fists to punch the big leather-and-wood chair in her office. I thought that was a stupid idea and I told her so.

"Humor me," she said.

So I gave it a half-hearted punch and sat back in my chair with a look on my face that practically shouted, "See? I'm not angry."

Then she said, "You can do a lot better than that if you put some muscle behind that fist, just like you do on the dry dock." Just as she intended, that comment came through as a dare; I hit harder. It felt very good.

"Go ahead," she said when I looked up at her in surprise. "Concentrate!"

And that's when I discovered that my right arm had a life of its own. Like a hydraulic pile driver on steroids, I punched that chair until I broke it in half.

I was astonished. "Well done," she said. "Now we can do some very good work together."

Gwen helped me see that holding all my feelings inside was making me emotionally rigid and keeping me stuck. We discovered that although running away helped me blow off steam when I was angry, it also kept me from acknowledging my feelings. My anger had been a motivating force in my life. Acknowledging it was my first step in learning to listen to it. Since I'd been so angry for so long, I had a lot of work to do.

Gwen taught me that anger is an emotion that's part of the human experience, and that feeling it is my birthright. Feeling angry and saying no are two behaviors that many women have been taught are not "feminine." Gwen taught me that both are essential for a healthy life.

Anger is simply my body's way of signaling dissatisfaction or disagreement to my brain so I can do something about it. Even though feeling my anger was a normal and healthy thing, acting on it was another matter altogether. I learned to be conscious in the ways I channeled it so I didn't bring harm to myself or others.

Thirty years after Gwen and her chair exercise—right after I'd used my inner Lion to climb that redwood tree at the ropes course in California—I discovered kick-boxing while working with Donald, a personal trainer, in Reston, Virginia. I nicknamed him "The Donald" because he was ruthless about helping me channel my feelings (including the unresolved anger I was carrying around after Chuck's recent bout with colon cancer and chemotherapy) into a focused force that left me feeling powerful and confident.

Since my work with Gwen and The Donald, I've learned a lot about my own power. I now have the instinct to seek out opportunities to grow, both professionally and personally. In 2005, however, I had another epiphany. Despite the growing number of distinctions, structures, and strategies I'd used to build a successful life for myself, I discovered that when faced with a very difficult situation, I still depended on running or fighting. There were still circumstances in which I became rigid. Clearly, I needed to lighten up.

Dancing was exactly what I needed.

Even though I had eliminated dancing as a possibility long ago (why try something I knew I did badly?), something inside of me was aching for it anyway. After investigating all the possibilities, I decided I'd have my greatest success with Middle Eastern dancing (what Westerners call "belly dancing").

My foray into dancing began at Visions of the Nile in Akron, Ohio. In my first few group lessons, I felt like Frankenstein's sister. My entire six-foot frame towered stiffly and awkwardly above my shorter classmates, all of whom had clearly taken years of ballet and tap growing up! They moved like dancers; I moved like I had just been sewn together with the body parts of various dead people. My feet were leaden—as if I was wearing heavy boots, and my spine was stiff—like I had a steel plate in it.

I was fifty-three years old. Knowing this was my last chance at dancing, I wasn't giving up.

Deciding to take private lessons with Ameenah, the owner of the studio, transformed the experience for me. She taught me baby steps first and praised me for everything I did well. With each lesson, I got better and better; Frankenstein's sister quickly disappeared. Soon I danced every day in my kitchen.

After a couple of months of weekly lessons, Ameenah told me something that changed my life. We'd been working together long enough for her to identify my dancing strengths, which turned out to be my hips and my legs. Once I'd relaxed enough to use them with ease in my practice, the natural power in my hips and legs allowed me to move with grace. I actually glided. As Ameenah pointed this out to me, she told me the secret of all great dancers: They always dance to their strengths! Every great dancer has five or six natural moves that she incorporates into each dance.

I'd been teaching people to play to their strengths for years, so that idea resonated with me deeply. You may have heard of these famous dancers who played to their signature strengths by creating their own dance forms: Isadora Duncan, Bob Fosse, and Michael Jackson. Instead of trying to fit themselves into the dances of their times, they used their natural abilities to create something new. Millions of others copied them.

Dancing gave me new ideas for dealing with the overwhelming emotion I still felt in the midst of difficult circumstances. Instead of running from my emotion or fighting it, I could dance with it. There's a dance for any emotion you feel: joy, anger, disappointment, sorrow, loneliness, love, enthusiasm, jealousy, or anything else. I discovered that if you can feel it, you can dance it. Pierre Dulaine taught me that "if you can walk, you can dance," and some very successful dancers on Broadway taught me that if you can STOMP, you can dance, too.

With dancing as the alternative to running away, I could stay with whatever difficulty arose and deal with my emotions in the flow of moving.

With dancing as the alternative to punching the air in frustration, I realized I was tapping in to strategies I'd learned from the martial art of aikido, which I had learned about in the early nineties.

Aikido is a form of fighting that is based on a deep sense of peace and love. Instead of fighting force with force, you move with the energy of the attack in a circular motion. You protect yourself by moving with the flow of the attack and dancing with it to move your attacker off balance so you can get away. Dancing with your attacker—what a concept!

Dancing is one of the most wonderful strategies I've ever learned, because life will bring you things you don't like when you least expect it. I've discovered that using your energy to dance with whatever comes your way increases your success and happiness.

How about you?

┌─ **Take Action** ──────────────────────────────────┐

Take a moment before reading any further and consider your experience with dancing. What has it been? What do you know about dancing that would help you to move gracefully through your challenges?

└──┘

Using the Strategy of Dancing

Now that you've been using the Three Empowering Beliefs for a while, you have a very good foundation for practicing this strategy. You know that you *bring about what you think about*, that *you have what it takes*, and that *every obstacle brings a gift*. These Three Empowering Beliefs help you *dance with whatever shows up*—dancing is impossible without them.

As always, there's a three-step strategy for developing this skill:

Step 1. Investigate the kind of dancer you are so you can identify your signature dancing strengths.

Step 2. Decide that dancing is an option you'll choose.

Step 3. Dance at every opportunity—in good circumstances as well as challenging ones—until dancing becomes a way of life for you.

Step 1: Investigate the Kind of Dancer You Are

The operative word here is *investigate!* No matter how long it takes you to feel comfortable dancing, stick with it. If you want to be a dancer, you will be, even if you're not sure it's possible when you start. Since my early experiences with dancing weren't positive, it took working with Ameenah to identify my signature dancing strengths. It made all the difference for me when I learned how to dance from a dancer.

One of the greatest benefits of one-on-one lessons was overturning the beliefs I had developed as a child about my dancing ability, which allowed me to override the ridicule I heard from some of the people who were important to me. Although it took some time to feel confident with it, by the time I got to belly dancing, I knew it was my last chance. Finally, my desire to do something I loved overrode my fears and doubts. I had to decide that I wanted to dance more than anything and that I was willing to do whatever it took.

How about you?

Take Action

What do you need to do to identify your dancing strengths? What kind of dancing calls to you? What would it take for you to sign up for some classes or lessons? Set a date for yourself and investigate. Report your progress in your journal.

Step 2: Decide That Dancing is an Option

Once you've identified your dancing strengths, it's a lot easier to decide to dance. This process takes as long as it takes, so be gentle with yourself if this is a big stretch for you. While you're investigating your own strengths, it's worthwhile to investigate the world of dancing in a way that makes sense to you. Getting excited about dancing is the first step in being willing to choose it for yourself.

You can also use the strategy of finding a role model, which we've used throughout this book. Who are your favorite dancers? Do you watch shows like *Dancing with the Stars*? Do you watch movies about dancing?

Immerse yourself in dancing with books, movies, and TV shows; bring dancing into your daily life. Remember that *you bring about what you think about*, so why not think about dancing?

When you're ready, take your first dancing step.

> **Take Action**
>
> Surround yourself with dancing until you're ready to choose it for yourself. Once you do, report your decision in your journal.

Step 3: Dance at Every Opportunity

Once you've decided to dance, you can choose to dance with everything. You can dance with your feet and you can dance with your mind.

Once you get the rhythm of dancing in your body, you'll find that you're developing the qualities of a dancer: flexibility and moving gracefully through space. When you focus on the moving and the grace, you're programming your RAS to help you filter for those qualities. You'll discover that just like identifying your dream car from the first Take Action exercise in Chapter 9, and looking for the gift hidden in every obstacle, it now becomes much easier to see those opportunities to dance that you may have missed before.

> **Take Action**
>
> Pay attention to your dancing opportunities. Have some fun with this—approach every situation with the idea that it's an invitation to dance. Record your findings in your journal as they occur.

Dance with Whatever Shows Up

During the January 2012 Journey to Powerful Presence teleclass, one of the Dancers, Louise, gave us a wonderful role model for dancing with whatever shows up.

She'd been watching all four of the *Pirates of the Caribbean* DVDs for the first time during the two weeks we'd been covering this topic. She told us she noticed that Captain Jack Sparrow is a master at dancing with whatever shows up. He's always ready, with flexibility and grace, for anything that happens. He seems to have a mindset that every situation he faces requires dancing. He moves like a dancer even when he walks, which helps him maneuver his way gracefully through whatever situation he encounters. She said that watching him dance through all his trials and tribulations helped her see how using dancing as a strategy would help her deal with her own challenges.

Everything you've learned so far will help you dance with your circumstances. Now that you have some experience with dancing, there are two more strategies that will exponentially increase your skill: saying *"Yes ... and"* and *pretending*.

Strategy #1: Say "Yes ... and"

This is a strategy I learned from my study of improvisational (improv) theater. Have you ever seen an improv troupe at work? If you have, you've seen what looks like a scripted and rehearsed play. Skilled improv actors make you forget that there is no script in improv. The play is actually being created second by second, by a group of people whose only tools are their highly focused Attention on each other and their willingness to say "Yes ... and" in every moment. Those two behaviors allow them to create magic for their audiences.

My theater training and my passion for improv gave me another strategy for increasing my Powerful Presence. When I took the "yes ... and" from improv and applied it to dealing with difficult circumstances, I found I could really dance.

When I climbed that redwood, even though I was scared, I said, "Yes, this tree is here for me to climb... and I'll do it my own way." Saying "yes ... and" allowed me to move through my fear and get up that tree. Without it, I would have been rooted to the spot.

My Powerful Presence role models from Part Four all said "Yes ... and" to their circumstances:

- "Yes, to this concentration camp … and I will still use my skills to spread hope."
- "Yes, to all of my disabilities … and I will still find my abilities."
- "Yes, I've been unjustly imprisoned … and I am the master of my fate, I am the captain of my ship in every waking hour."

The important thing about "yes … and" is that it doesn't require you to agree. It requires that you get into 3rd Gear and catch whatever's been thrown your way. Once you accept it, you can contribute to it. On the stage, that's called *co-creating the scene*. You can co-create your circumstances by adding "yes … and" to anything that happens to you. When you're co-creating, you're dancing into your power—no matter what circumstances you face.

When you use "yes … and" as a strategy of Powerful Presence, you accept the spot you're in and use your resources to address it. Those resources include:

- shifting Gears
- tapping in to the Three Empowering Beliefs
- using the Clock Face Technique
- seeing yourself in the mirror by looking in your own eyes
- using the Best Friend Technique
- *walking your talk with integrity*: investigate, decide, and act
- relating to others: focus your Attention, match the other person's style, and address listening barriers

Just like using aikido, when you *dance with whatever shows up* you move with it instead of against it. You use your energy to move with the flow of your life instead of trying to stop it or fight it. Saying "Yes … and" allows you to get creative about it.

It's important to make a distinction between saying yes to your circumstances and saying yes to requests from other people. You still have 10 yeses a day to spend; saying yes to the circumstances of your life means spending some of them. When you're facing difficulties, it's not usually possible to say no to the situation in the same way you can when a request comes from a person.

When you're conscious of where you're spending your yeses and nos, you can often say no to requests that have the potential to bring you negative results. If you don't do that up front, then the best way to work through the difficulties that result is to say "Yes ... and," so you can address them.

One Caveat

"Yes ... and" is very different from "Yes ... but." Grammatically, the word *but* cancels anything that comes before it. That phrase is a *no* posing as a yes.

When you say "Yes ... but," you're not dancing, you're just getting yourself stuck. The circumstances you're facing have happened whether you like it or not. When you say "Yes ... but," you waste energy pointing to the ways the other person is wrong or the situation isn't fair, or the reasons it's not your fault.

"Yes ... but" has no power to it and saying it wastes everyone's time.

When you say "Yes ... and" to your circumstances, you save your energy for the "and." That's where you have power and creativity; just like the actors in improv, you can create magic in your life with it.

Take Action

When can you say "Yes ... and" to dance with a situation you currently face? Try it—and note your results in your journal.

Although saying "Yes ... and" is a very powerful strategy, sometimes you need another strategy to dance with something that challenges you. Sometimes you need to pretend.

Strategy #2: Pretend

Have you ever noticed that little kids have an astonishing ability to bend their reality in a positive way by pretending?

If you've ever been around a child who's doing it, you know you're experiencing an alternate reality. Whatever a child is pretending is completely real for her; it's the truth in her 1st Gear. It's also the biological foundation of her ability to learn. Little kids are masters at the practice of "act as if," and they always imagine themselves as the masters of their universe.

Bill Watterson reminded me of this when I was introduced to his comic strip, *Calvin and Hobbes*, in 1987. Meeting those two characters reconnected me to the six-year-old I had been: A Faerie Princess full of magic and Light—the mistress of all I surveyed in the books in which I immersed myself. *Calvin and Hobbes* reminded me that when life hands you something you don't like, you can transmogrify it and turn it into something you like better. Although the word was first coined in 1656 and means "to alter or change something, often in a grotesque or humorous way," *Calvin and Hobbes* proved to me that transmogrify is just another word for "imagining your circumstances in a positive way." This is a strategy I've claimed as my own.

Have you ever noticed how great most adults are at the negative version of pretending: "What if this is a disaster?" "What if I'm not good enough?" "What if everything I've planned falls apart?" Most adults find that using their imagination this way is often the foundation of their getting stuck!

Here's the good news: You don't have to keep doing that. You can use your natural skill for pretending to turn your circumstances around from disaster to delight.

All you have to do is switch your focus. Use the beliefs of Powerful Presence to reprogram your RAS; filter in the available opportunities to be master of your own universe, just like you did when you were a kid. Use your imagination as the foundation of your learning so you can expand your range of skills and build your repertoire of responses in a positive way.

In my case, pretending I was strong got me up that redwood; pretending I know what I'm doing has kept me in business for over twenty-two years!

When you use pretending as a strategy to dance with whatever shows up, you use everything you've learned so far on this Journey to create an amazing life for yourself in which you are happy and resourceful.

Try it for yourself by using the two most powerful creativity-triggering words: what if? Research indicates—and my experience with myself and my clients has proved to me—that these words are the equivalent of "Open Sesame" to your reticular activating system.

Here's how it works: Start with the belief that *you bring about what you think about*. Depending on the challenge you're facing, use one of the questions below to engage in child-like pretending:

1. What if I *had* what it takes right now?
2. What if there *is* a gift in this obstacle?
3. What if I *was* walking my talk with integrity right now—what would I do?
4. What if I *could* relate to this person with skill and ease—what would I do?

The more you pretend, the better you get!

Consider Malcolm Gladwell's idea that it takes 10,000 hours of practice at something in order to master it. Where have you spent your 10,000 hours of pretending so far? If you've spent it imagining disasters, you know how well you've mastered pretending in its negative form. Get started right now on your 10,000 hours of pretending like a child and see how quickly your life transforms.

Take Action

What situation are you facing right now that you've pretended is a disaster? What else could you pretend is true about it now? Remember that you bring about what you think about, so choose something positive to pretend. See what happens when you do and record your findings in your journal.

Dancing Happens in the Present Moment

Now that you have all these strategies for dancing, it ought to be a cinch to start doing it on a regular basis, right? That's the question that lies at the very heart of our Journey.

If dancing is so easy, why isn't everybody doing it? That's the question we'll answer in the next chapter.

Chapter 18

The Dancer's Treasure

*D*ancing *with whatever shows* up is easy when you know how to stay in the present moment.

Learning how to stay in the present moment has been the true purpose of your Journey. Although it's taken most of the trip to arrive here, it was the only way you could discover the treasure that's been waiting for you. The Dancer's Treasure is the ability to dance into your own power whenever you want to, because you finally understand that you only have power over yourself.

You can only access this power when you stay
in the present moment; that's what allows you to
dance with whatever shows up.

Even though you might not have been aware of it, staying in the present moment is something you've already done as you've progressed through this Journey. Any time you were taking action, you were in the present moment.

For example, remember when you asked someone who loves you what they see in you that you don't? When you listened, you were in the present moment. When you used any of the strategies in this book—like the Clock Face Technique or the Best Friend Technique—to shift your state, you were in the present moment. And when you recorded your thoughts in you journal, you were in the present moment.

Now that you know the secret of the Dancer's Treasure, here are the hallmarks of being in the present moment:

1. Your Attention is outside of you.
2. Your breathing is typically deep and rhythmic—unless you're doing something very physical.
3. You're able to shift into the Gear that best suits the circumstances.

Take Action

Catch yourself being in the present moment. Go back and look through the entries you've made in your journal. Look for the times when you were present based on the hallmarks above. What did you find? Capture your impressions in your journal.

Now that you know the hallmarks of being in the present moment, it's just as important to uncover the things that stop you from *dancing with whatever shows up*. That's the only way you'll have the choice to overcome them. As you overcome them, you'll increase your ability to dance into your power.

What Stops You from Dancing?

To paraphrase Tom Hanks, "If dancing was easy, everyone would be doing it!" It is never easy to dance, especially at the beginning. There are times when we get stopped by what shows up. Sometimes we only get stopped a little; other times we get stopped a lot. Stopping is not a problem as long as you remember that you have the choice to dance.

When I ask my clients and the Dancers in my classes, "What stops you?" it doesn't take long to uncover the answer. The biggest obstacle that limits our ability to *dance with whatever shows up* is our expectations.

When you have an expectation about something, you assume it's going to happen. Your expectations are based on your beliefs, values, opinions, and experiences. Since your beliefs program your reticular activating system, can you see how your expectations are now a part of your filter? Expectations happen in 1st Gear; they're the truth for you.

There's nothing wrong with having expectations—until what you expect doesn't happen. Then you have a choice: you can *dance with whatever showed up*, or you can get stuck in the disparity between what you wanted to happen and what actually did.

When we get stuck because of our unmet expectations, we can't dance. You won't be surprised to discover that there are three sources of this problem:

1. getting stuck in the past
2. getting stuck in the future
3. mistaking things you have no power over for things you do have power over

Let's explore them separately.

Source #1: Getting Stuck in the Past

When you get stuck in the past, you can't distinguish the present moment from some moment in the past that was emotionally overpowering for you.

It's funny that although people often get stuck in a negative emotion from their past, they never seem to get stuck in a positive one. Positive moments in the past serve to motivate us or support us or soothe us when we need it the most. I've learned that we all remember the past. Now I know how to use the past to remember the good that's happened to me. I teach my clients to use that strategy, too.

When I feel stuck, I have a strategy to assess my state as well as to address what's happening with me. I discovered this strategy through years of trial and error. As a result, there are several layers to it. It was only after I started teaching it to my clients and watched them get positive results with it that I realized how powerful it is. As you read through the two strategies below, you will see several elements that you've already learned. All I'm doing is combining them.

Strategy #1: Assess and Address

When I get stuck, I have three distinctions to help me assess my state and discover what's really happening. I ask myself these three questions:

1. Where is your Attention?
2. Do you have a BEPPUMOID?
3. What Gear are you in?

Just asking these questions usually stops me dead in my tracks and shifts my state—so I can remember that I have the choice to dance. Sometimes that's all it takes. Once I've shifted, I can laugh at myself for making a mountain out of a molehill, and dance through it with gratitude for these distinctions and my own Powerful Presence.

There are other times when it's not so easy. When I really get stuck in the past, I get hooked on old triggers that I have not cleared. That's when I have to slow things down and allow each question to help me clear the emotional debris from my past. So I ask myself these questions one at a time, taking one action before I move to the next question.

1. Where is your Attention?
   a. When I'm stuck, my Attention is on me, so I'm effectively closed off from getting any input from anyone else. No one can help me right now. I'm stuck inside the past.
   b. The action required: I have to shift my Attention off myself, even if I can only put it onto my cat, Fionn. Shifting my Attention helps me loosen the grip of my emotion so I can ask the next question.

2. Do you have a BEPPUMOID?
   a. When I'm stuck remembering something from my past that holds high emotion for me, I've just developed a BEPPUMOID infestation. I can no longer hear anything in the present because my emotion keeps me deaf and blind to anything but my past experience. It's just like having one of those "mind-altering eels" in my head.
   b. The action required: I have to handle the symptoms. When I'm physically or mentally tired, I find that I get emotional more easily. Before I take any action about what has upset me, I have to sleep and eat; I just have to pause and take care of myself. Often a night's sleep and a meal will eradicate my BEPPUMOIDs so I can investigate what had me so emotional the day before.

3. What Gear are you in?
   a. When I'm stuck, I'm in 1st Gear, and my past experience is the only truth for me in the present.
   b. The action required: I have to shift myself to neutral until I can get into 3rd Gear and explore the circumstances with logic. I have to be able to see the whole situation—above and beyond where I got stuck. This practice of getting into 3rd Gear has helped me create a number of distinctions over the years and create some very effective strategies.

Let me give you an example of a situation in which I got stuck in the past and what I did about it:

When Chuck and I were first married, there were times when I did things that annoyed him. This was easy enough to do, since I'm a *quick/relationship* person and he's a *careful/task* person. To add to the excitement, we were working together in my business and we were just discovering how to communicate effectively with each other. We hadn't yet learned how to play to our strengths.

The intention behind Chuck's response to my behavior was to help me change what I was doing—to be more effective or efficient; my response to him was anger. My anger connected me to my past—to those times in my family when I got yelled at or put down for just being myself—and I got stuck. Only when I took the time to get into 3rd Gear and think about it did I realize that there was a structure to my getting stuck in the past. Using my three distinctions it was clear to me that:

1. My Attention was on me and how I felt. Since I felt like Chuck was the man of my dreams, my intention was to be the perfect wife for him; my expectation was that nothing I ever did would frustrate or annoy him. Despite my best intentions, anything other than the warm tone of voice he usually had for me would send me into the past. (He was my third husband! It was alarming to me that I could frustrate him as much as I did. I took it personally instead of chalking it up to the normal growing pains of a new relationship.)

2. I was emotional and I was reconnecting to the pain I felt in my family. I definitely had a full-blown BEPPUMOID infestation: EMOTIONAL!

3. I was in 1st Gear, so everything I felt was the truth for me. I felt so awful, I couldn't shift into 2nd or 3rd. (This was before I created "neutral.")

Over time we realized that there was a pattern of things I did that were frustrating for Chuck and there was a pattern to the way I responded when he tried to approach me about them. Although we couldn't talk about them in the heat of the moment, we made it a point to revisit them when we were both more resourceful and could explore the situation in 3rd Gear. We both wanted to solve the mystery; neither of us could figure out what got me so angry.

Finally, in a class I was taking, I learned a very powerful NLP question: "When have you ever felt like this before?" which allowed me to discover the unconscious structure I had for conflict and tone of voice.

Once I connected my feelings to the past in 3rd Gear, it was easy to see that the past situation was very different from the current situation. Once I unhooked myself from the anger of my past, I became more able to stay in the present with Chuck when we had differences. Making this distinction inspired me to map out the actions required to shift myself when I got stuck.

We've been practicing the "assess and address" strategy for so many years now that neither of us gets stuck in the past for long. We've both gotten very skilled at snapping out of the past and into the present because we created a new structure for working through our differences.

Most people find that getting stuck in the past is very easy to do. You can make it just as easy to snap out of it when you are conscious about it when it happens. My three distinctions have helped my clients and me do just that.

It's impossible to release the past when you're still in it. That's why my strategy for "assess and address" is so useful. I can get caught up in negative emotions just like anyone else—I still have emotional triggers that affect me in a negative way. This strategy helps me check my state and then choose to be present to what's happening to me.

Once I'm clear that I've gotten stuck in the past, I have another strategy to work my way through it so I can finally release it. This strategy helps me release it so it can never trigger me again.

Strategy #2: Release the Past

These three steps have helped me—and my clients—strategically sort through emotional situations that previously kept us trapped in the past:

Step 1. **Ask yourself: "When have I felt this way before?"** Since your Attention is on you, use it to your advantage and investigate your emotion. Pinpoint exactly what the emotion is: fear, anger, dread, sorrow, frustration, anxiety, rage—or something else.

Step 2. **Ask yourself: "What's the pattern?"** Keep asking yourself this question and follow the clues until you discover where they lead. See if you can identify the pattern all the way back to its first occurrence. Odds are high that you were very young the first time you experienced it; that's why it's so emotional and so painful. Ask yourself: "What do I know now that I didn't know as a child?" When you discover this, it will help you release this trigger. When I use this question with my clients, they find out just how much power they have in the present. Together, we use that power to heal the past.

Step 3. **Release the past.** Once you find the pattern, do everything you can to handle your feelings so you can release this experience. This might take you more than one try, so have patience with yourself and keep asking yourself, "What's the pattern?" until you're satisfied that you've found the root answer. When you release the past, you update your reticular activating system and your 1st Gear. The more you release the past, the better able you are to live in the present moment.

Take Action

When was the last time you got stuck in the past? What happened? In your journal, map it out using the "release the past" strategy above. What did you discover? What do you need to do to release that past experience? Do what you need to do and record your progress in your journal.

Source #2: Getting Stuck in the Future

When you're stuck in the past, you're hooked to something that's already happened that you haven't released.

When you're stuck in the future, you're so focused on something that you want to happen, or that you're afraid will happen, that you can't take the steps in the present to make sure that it does— or doesn't. You might be spending money you haven't earned yet because you can see that raise coming; you might be so worried that your relationship will end that you don't engage with your partner in ways that will build or protect it.

Getting stuck in the future prevents you from living in the present because you've moved into the future before it arrives. Three things are happening:

1. **Where is your Attention?** Your Attention is on you and your thoughts of your future, whether they're positive or negative.
2. **Do you have a BEPPUMOID?** You're feeling high emotion, either positive or negative. You're also distracted and preoccupied with your vision of how things are going to be. Now you've got a serious BEPPUMOID infestation and you can't get any input from anyone else.
3. **What Gear are you in?** You're in 1st Gear; what you're experiencing is the truth for you.

Although getting stuck in the future seems to be less prevalent for most of my clients, it's still a difficult place to find yourself. Although getting stuck in the past has been one of my greatest challenges on this Journey, working with clients who've gotten stuck in the future helped me see that there was a time when I did that, too.

When I was in my twenties, I would get stuck focusing on a future that I believed would only be worse than my present. It was so bleak that I felt bad every time I thought about it. Looking back on it now, I can see that I alternated between stuck in the past and stuck in the future—until the pain I felt helped me decide that I wanted something else. Working with Gwen Nichols got me started on my Journey to Powerful Presence. Many years later, while working with my own clients, I created the antidote below to help them get unstuck when they got caught in a negative expectation of the future.

Although the context is different, this is the same "assess and address" strategy I use to shift myself when I get stuck in the past.

1. **Where is your Attention?** I had to shift my Attention from my own grim vision of a future so I could pay attention to people like my Powerful Presence role models, who created miracles in circumstances much worse than mine. My current life didn't match the miserable future I was focused on, and I had lots of help and support building a better future for myself. You'll find the story I wrote about this process in the Epilogue.

2. **Do you have a BEPPUMOID?** I had to handle my Emotional, Preoccupied, and Distracted BEPPUMOIDs so I could hear the distinctions, structures, and strategies I needed to build a better future for myself. I had to learn to be a better listener.

3. **What Gear are you in?** I had to learn to shift Gears and find neutral; I had to keep checking my progress from the perspective of each Gear; I had to adapt my behavior. Considering my circumstances from 3rd Gear with my

counselors and teachers allowed me to make different choices and create a future for myself that is rewarding and fulfilling.

Now that you know how to use the "assess and address" strategy, use it on yourself until you're ready to dig deeper. Below is the strategy I use with my clients to prepare for a positive and rewarding future.

My Strategy: Prepare for the Future

These three steps have helped me—and my clients—strategically sort through emotional situations that previously kept us trapped in the future:

1. **Check your Attention: Where is it?**
   a. Shift it off yourself and onto your current circumstances. What is really happening for you right now? Do your current circumstances match your future daydream?
   b. Do a reality check so you can see how close you are to what you want—or how far away you are from what you don't want.
   c. Pay attention to everything that's happening around you and decide what action you can take right now to get what you want—or to avoid what you don't.

2. **Check your BEPPUMOIDs:**
   a. Identify your symptoms.
   b. Handle them.
   c. Listen for yourself: What action can you take right now to create the future you want and avoid the one you don't?

3. **Shift Gears:**
   a. Get out of 1st Gear and into neutral as quickly as you can.
   b. As soon as you can do it, shift into 3rd Gear to consider all the available possibilities without emotion so you can discover your best options.

c. Check your options from 1st Gear and pick one. Get into action with something you can do right now to prepare for the future you want.

Everything you've learned on this Journey will help you prepare for the future of your dreams. You just have to be willing to pay attention and adjust your behavior.

Take Action

When was the last time you got stuck in the future? What happened? In your journal, map it out using the strategy above. What did you discover? What do you need to do to prepare for the future you want? Do what you need to do to adjust your vision of your future and continue to record your progress in your journal.

Now that you've seen how you can get stuck in the past and the future, there's only one more obstacle to your dancing.

Source #3: Mistaking Things You Have No Power Over for Things You Do Have Power Over

Now that you've travelled this far on your Journey, how would you answer this question:

How can you tell the difference between those things you have power over and those things you don't have power over?

If you answered that you only have power over *yourself*, congratulations! It wasn't just something you read.

This next distinction will help you get exceptionally skilled at dancing into your power. I learned it while designing and instructing a leadership course that I co-authored with a colleague several years ago. Although I learned it in the context of time management, it translates perfectly to the belief that you only have power over yourself. What follows is my version of it.

Every circumstance you'll face in life will fall into four distinct categories:

1. **Things you can do something about:** everything that has to do with your beliefs, values, opinions, experiences, and behavior
2. **Things you can't do anything about:** everything that involves someone else
3. **When you can do something about it and you don't:** you *lose* your power
4. **When you can't do anything about it and you try to:** you *have* no power

---
┌ Take Action ───────────────────────

Consider a situation in your life that's frustrating you so much that you can't dance with it. Into which of these four categories does it fall? What's one action you could take about it right now that would help you dance into your power? Capture your thoughts in your journal.

The Dancer in You

Now you have everything you need to start dancing.

You know that life brings you things you like and things you don't like. The most powerful way to engage with your life is to dance with it using the distinctions, structures, and strategies you've learned on this Journey:

- Use the Three Empowering Beliefs to stay positive.
- Use the three Gears to shift your perspective.
- Focus your Attention where it will help you the most.
- Keep developing your ability to walk your talk with integrity.
- Keep developing your ability to relate to others.

- Say "Yes... and."
- Pretend like a child.

When you get stuck in the past or the future, or you mistake something you can't do anything about for something you can, use the antidotes you just learned to overcome those obstacles you encounter along the way. Then keep dancing.

Congratulations! You've just completed Part Four of this book. You've gotten a start on your lifelong Journey of developing and refining the Three Resourceful Abilities that make up Powerful Presence:

- Walk your talk with integrity.
- Relate to others.
- Dance with whatever shows up.

We've almost completed our Journey together. Now that you're here, I hope you'll take the time to celebrate your accomplishments. Take a look at your journal and see how far you've come. The rest of your life's Journey stretches out ahead of you; it will be different now because of the Journey that lies behind you.

As always, no great journey happens without periods of rest and relaxation. We're almost at the end of our time together, so I hope you'll take the time now to savor where we've been. Do something really nice for yourself, and wait at least twenty-four hours before you start Part Five.

Celebrate!

Part Five

Three Focused Actions

Dance into Your Power

Chapter 19

Taking the Three Focused Actions

A ction is the trademark of knowledge. Without it, everything you've learned becomes irrelevant.

Now that you know how to dance into your power, we'll spend the rest of our Journey focused on ways you can continue to dance. Dancing requires action. In this section, we'll explore three specific strategies for staying in action long after you've closed this book.

Before we go any further, let's get on the same page about the word action. No matter what source you choose, all its definitions point to three important distinctions:

1. Action is a conscious process.
2. Action happens over time.
3. Action requires movement.

The distinctions, structures, and strategies that I've shared with you in this book took time to discover and develop. Much of it was a process of trial and error—with lots of error! It was a process that required me to keep moving forward on this Journey so I could change and grow. I had to keep using what I'd learned until I'd mastered it—only then could I share what I knew. As a result, I created something new.

Every action you took before you got to this page has changed you. Every action you take once you put this book down will keep those changes alive. Every action you take will help you continue to grow.

In this section, you'll see how the Three Focused Actions will help you do that. You'll learn how to:

- Use what you've learned.
- Share what you know.
- Create something new.

By now you've watched me break down all the pieces of this Journey into three steps, or three strategies, or a three-part structure; there's a 1-2-3 to everything we've explored. I've discovered that just about everything in life can be broken down into manageable actions using that same structure.

Once you're willing to break anything down into three pieces like that, you can accomplish things you never dreamed possible. Once you begin to think like that, you'll find that you've created three steps that will help you dance through anything, just like the 1-2-3 of a waltz.

One version of a three-step structure that we've used throughout this Journey is the Gears. In the last section, we mapped the structure of the Three Resourceful Abilities using the three Gears. They also provide us with the perfect structure with which to map out the Three Focused Actions.

- 1st Gear: **Use what you've learned.** The beliefs and abilities you've discovered on this Journey will only serve you when you use them. Once you finish reading this book, keep using your journal; revisit your Journey periodically and capture every opportunity you've taken to use what you know. Stay conscious of your actions—and stay curious. Developing your Powerful Presence is an intentional practice that you build over time. Just like learning the steps of a new dance, the more you practice, the better you get. And the more you practice, the easier it gets.

- 2nd Gear: **Share what you know.** The best way to learn something is to share it with someone else. People who love you will wonder what you're doing when they see the changes in you. When you share what you're doing and where you learned it, you increase the amount of Powerful Presence in the world. Just imagine the possibilities!

- 3rd Gear: **Create something new.** This book is the result of my synthesizing all the things I learned in a way that only I could. This Journey is the result of my particular experiences; your Journey is the result of yours. When you take the time to synthesize the things you've learned along the way, you'll be amazed by what you can create. Being in action helps you be creative; playing to your strengths helps you find the gift that only you can bring to the world.

Before we continue, it's worth addressing something you may have already guessed. As I mentioned in Part Four, abilities take longer to develop than beliefs take to choose. As you've been doing throughout your Journey, taking action helps you develop your abilities. Being in action is a lifelong activity that will take you places you can't even imagine right now.

Being in action for your Powerful Presence is the practice of dancing into your power every day. Ask any dancer what it takes to be world-class and she will tell you, "Practice dancing every day."

World-class dancers have mastered what new and developing dancers strive for—dancing as an instinct.

In the next three chapters, you'll discover a structure you can use to make dancing into your power *your* instinct.

Chapter 20

Action #1: Use What You've Learned

Taking a journey to anyplace changes you. You're not the same person who set out on that journey—you've been affected by all that you've seen and heard and done.

Imagine that you're almost at the end of a journey that you've really enjoyed. In another few days, you'll be heading home. What would be the most important thing for you to do right now?

Most people tell me that at the end of a remarkable journey they aren't quite ready to go home. They want to stretch out their last day or two and drink in everything around them so they can take as much of it with them as possible. If you've ever traveled to someplace you thought was magical, you know exactly what I mean.

As much as you might be tempted to keep traveling, one thing is certain for all journeys: No matter where you've gone, the journey always ends.

When you take some time to consider where you've been, you can make some plans about what you want to do next. Get the most enjoyment out of the process by consciously making the transition from traveling to being back home.

Now that you've learned the distinctions, structures, and strategies of Powerful Presence, all that's left is for you to put them into action in your life. At this point, I ask my clients and the Dancers who take this class with me this question:

> *What's one action you can take right now*
> *that will help you put into daily practice*
> *the distinctions, structures, and strategies*
> *you've learned on this Journey?*

The answer I almost always get is, "Plan for it."

This has been a long Journey with a lot of discoveries. To get the best answer to that question, let's take a moment to consider where you've been so you can create a plan for yourself.

Where Have You Been?

When we first started this Journey together, you took the time to pack an essential travel accessory—the Gears—and you created an itinerary for yourself.

We've used the Gears throughout this Journey. Now how can you continue to use them in your life? If you want to make it really simple, keep up the practice of changing Gears that you started when we began this Journey.

Once you've decided how you can use the Gears going forward, take a moment to review your itinerary and see whether you reached the destination you set for yourself.

When you take this Journey with me as a teleclass or a live class, we spend thirty minutes reviewing your itinerary together. You can certainly do the same thing with someone you trust. If you created your itinerary with someone's help when we first started, make an appointment with that person and go over it together. You'll be astonished at how much you've accomplished if you've been taking action all along and recording your progress in your journal.

Now that you've addressed the Gears and your itinerary, take a look at the rest of your Journey. Here's where you'll find the background for the success you discovered when you reviewed your itinerary. If you'd been in class with me, this would have taken you eight of the twelve weeks of the Journey.

You've explored the Three Empowering Beliefs. Now you know that you can choose to believe that:

1. You bring about what you think about.
2. You have what it takes.
3. Every obstacle brings a gift.

You've explored the Three Resourceful Abilities. Now you know how to develop your ability to:

1. Walk your talk with integrity.
2. Relate to others.
3. Dance with whatever shows up.

Consider Your Progress

Before you can *use what you've learned,* you need a 3rd Gear assessment of your progress.

1. Ask yourself, "What's easier now? What used to be challenging that is no longer?"
2. Ask yourself, "What challenges do I still have?
3. Imagine yourself standing on a mountaintop, surveying the Journey you took to climb to this peak. You can see for miles; you have a 360 degree view. What can you see now that was invisible to you before you started this Journey? *(That's your reticular activating system at work!)*

When it comes right down to it, you'll always be in progress as long as you continue to act. You'll make mistakes you can learn from, you'll fall on your face so you can make more discoveries, and you'll have huge successes. That's just life.

Once you've taken the Journey to Powerful Presence, you become more conscious of your actions and your impact. That makes all the difference in your progress—it can actually speed it up because now you have a structure to it.

The Structure of Being Conscious of Your Actions and Your Impact

Have you ever heard of Stephen Covey's Circles of Concern and Influence? In his book *The Seven Habits of Highly Effective People,* Mr. Covey made two distinctions that I've never forgotten. He described two concentric circles: the Circle of Concern is the outside circle and the Circle of Influence is contained inside the Circle of Concern.

- In your Circle of Concern are all the things you're worried about or concerned about, yet can't personally affect, like world peace, the Middle East situation, politics, "kids these days," and so on. You may remember these kinds of things described in Chapter 18 as the "things you can't do anything about" because they involve other people's behavior.

- In the Circle of Influence are all those things you can personally affect: your behavior, your interactions, your beliefs, your values, your opinions, and your experiences. You may remember these kinds of things described in Chapter 18 as the "things you can do something about" because they're about you.

- Covey says that when your Circle of Influence is as large as possible, it's because you're taking more conscious action in the world. As a result, you have more impact—no matter what your circumstances.

Because I'm a highly visual person who synthesizes everything I learn into something personal, I've adapted Covey's two circles into a three-circle bull's-eye.

At the very center of these three concentric circles is a red circle that represents the things I can do that are also the things that matter the most to my success. They're the things I identified in Chapter 15 in my personal 10 Commandments.

My goal is not to expand my Circle of Influence; my goal is to deepen my success by using my "10 yeses a day" strategy to do what only I can do on the planet. For me that's like hitting a bull's-eye every day. It's the basis of the successful life I've learned to build for myself, and it's at the heart of Powerful Presence.

The Bull's-eye in Action

When I first learned about the Circles of Influence and Concern, I learned them in a supervisory course that I was helping a government agency redesign. Cynthia, the woman who was presenting the leadership portion of the supervisory course, used the story of Flight 93 to illustrate the ways in which those two circles worked. None of us who heard her that day will ever forget the impact of her story or her Powerful Presence as she told it.

Although you may never have thought of it this way before, I believe that the actions of the passengers on Flight 93 are the epitome of

Powerful Presence. Each of them was conscious of their actions and their impact, even though those were the last ones they took in life. Their impact is part of our history. Although they are no longer with us, the memory of who they were and what they did will live on through generations.

They focused on their bull's-eye to take action—and they changed the course of history.

No matter what their 1st Gear was at the time, we remember them for being able to move through it and shift into 2nd as they thought of their families and the people in this country, and then shift into 3rd as they took focused non-emotional action to commandeer that plane.

The passengers on Flight 93 focused on the things they *were able to do*—that *only they* could do—and then they got into action.

Take Action

Take a moment and reflect on your thoughts about this chapter. What can you do to create a bull's-eye of your own that will help you use what you've learned on this Journey? Capture your thoughts in your journal and take one action in the next twenty-four hours that will help you dance into your power.

When you *use what you've learned*, you bring it alive in your life. When you bring it alive, other people will notice it. How do you share what you know with them? That's the topic of the next chapter.

Chapter 21

Action #2: Share What You Know

Have you ever caught up with a friend you hadn't seen in a while and noticed that she'd changed in a very positive way that you couldn't quite put your finger on? What was the first thing you wanted to ask her after reconnecting and catching up on important details of your lives?

Most people tell me that the first thing they'd ask is something like, "Where have you been? What have you been doing? Whatever it is, it looks great on you!" You can tell when someone you care about has changed.

Now think about what your friend says when trying to explain what she's experienced to you. She's kind of vague, isn't she? She can tell you in general terms what she's been doing, yet she can't really share all the details with you unless you've been through a similar experience.

The same is true about your Journey to Powerful Presence.

People who know you have seen a change in you. Odds are high that you listen better now and you have some other new behaviors that are positive as well. How can you share everything you've been through on your Journey with someone who's never heard of it?

The good news is that you can share this book with them—and I hope you will. It's also important to recognize that not everyone you know will be ready to read this book at exactly the moment that you want to share it with them, so you have to have an alternative way to share what you know in a way they can hear it.

Fortunately, you have all the distinctions, structures, and strategies to share what you know from the perspective of 2nd Gear. Let's use the Gears as our first distinction as you consider your most effective way to share it:

- In your 1st Gear, you're so delighted about the results you've gotten from the work you've done that you can't wait to tell everyone you know about it. Now that you've taken this Journey, you know that telling everyone about it right now is only one possibility, so you slow yourself down and consider the other two. You want to make sure that you share what you know in a way that will benefit the other person.

- When you shift into 2nd Gear, you think about the person you're talking to and you consider whether this is the best time to share it with her. Has she asked you a question that you can answer by sharing something you know? Would that something you know truly benefit her in this moment? Every time you can answer yes to those questions, proceed with your sharing. As they say in the sales world, no one likes to be sold, yet everyone loves to buy! When the person you're with is looking for something you know, it's stunningly simple to share it. Look for those opportunities and you'll be amazed by your results.

- When you shift into 3rd Gear, you can look back to the time when you first heard about Powerful Presence or when you first picked up this book. Think of all the things you didn't know yet and the amount of time it took you to work through all the layers of each of the distinctions, structures, and strategies in this book. Imagine trying to share all of this with someone over coffee — it would be overwhelming! When you look at everything you've learned, you can see that you learned it in the same way you might eat a whole pizza: one bite at a time. You can only share it with someone else in the same way.

- Give yourself the opportunity to shift into neutral when the person you're speaking with isn't interested in your experience with Powerful Presence right now. Wait to share it until it would benefit her to hear it.

Can you see how using the Gears will help you share what you know?

There are at least two other distinctions that will help you share what you know: focus your Attention and check for BEPPUMOIDs.

1. **Focus your Attention:** When you focus your Attention on the other person, it will be obvious whether what you know is what she needs. When what you know flows easily in conversation as a result of the rapport between the two of you, it will be easy to engage her in hearing about your discoveries.

2. **Check for BEPPUMOIDs:** When you detect a BEPPUMOID of any sort in the other person, trying to share anything about Powerful Presence will be fruitless. Let her off the hook until she can hear you; use what you know about the Gears and Attention to do it in a way that works for both of you.

And finally, the best way to *share what you know* is to live it. Live it in such a way that other people notice the difference and want to know what you're up to!

Now that you know how to *use what you've learned* and *share what you know*, the possibility exists that you can *create something new* because of your Journey. That's the topic of the next chapter.

Chapter 22

Action #3: Create Something New

Years from now, you'll know more than you do now about what you can create in the world as a result of taking this Journey.

Right now your Journey is still fresh; the road to your future lies ahead of you. One thing I can promise is that your future will wait for you. By that I mean that it's always out there; it's always a possibility that's affected by the actions you take in the present.

Have you ever heard that when you're using a compass to plot your course, even a slight difference in degree of the angle of your travel can bring you to a completely different place? That's how I feel about my own Journey. It's astonishing to me that the trajectory of my travel since I left my home at seventeen has brought me to this place, to this work—and to this book. Yet it did.

My Journey to Powerful Presence took me over forty years. There were so many junctures where I had to choose my direction.

Sometimes I realized I was headed the wrong way. Many times I had to start over.

It's my belief that you and I are not very different when it comes to our Journeys. Sure, there are probably a lot of details about our lives that are different. Yet in our essence, I believe that each of us is living on this planet because we have a particular gift that the world needs. Our mission is to discover what that is and contribute it.

Yes, that was very 1st Gear of me … and … I simply offer it as a possibility for you to explore. Others before me have suggested this possibility:

- **Aristotle:** "Where your talents and the needs of the world cross, there lies your vocation."
- **Erica Jong:** "Everyone has talent. What is rare is the courage to follow the talent to the … place where it leads."
- **Winston Churchill:** "To every man there comes in his lifetime that special moment when he is figuratively tapped on the shoulder and offered the chance to do a very special thing, unique to him and fitted to his talents. What a tragedy if that moment finds him unprepared or unqualified for the work which could be his finest hour."

The idea that each of us is on the planet for a particular purpose is not a new one. You won't be surprised to find out that the first person I heard it from was Gwen Nichols—in 1978.

At one point in our work together, she told me that it was critical that I do everything in my power to have a successful life. She told me this was very important not only for me—it was important for someone in my future. She said that this person was waiting for me because she needed to hear something that only I could share. Gwen told me that if I didn't discover it, then an important message would be lost for both of us.

That was a potent vision that I took to heart. Although I couldn't foresee this future, I believed in Gwen. When somebody lets you break a chair in her office and then smiles at you like you've just won the Olympics, she is clearly someone of extraordinary power.

The seed she planted in me about discovering my particular gift grew into all the work I've done since 1987 when I began creating and teaching my own programs. It's the very root of Powerful Presence.

Now that you know about it, let me invite you to plant this seed in your own life. Even if you have no idea what your gift could be, don't worry. Clearly, based on my experience, knowing your gift at the beginning isn't necessary. All it takes to start is a willingness to trust in the possibility.

In the meantime, congratulate yourself on all the work you've done on your Journey. My guess is that you've transformed your present in ways you may not see until your future unfolds.

Let me assure you that—like Gwen—I believe with all my heart that someone is waiting in your future to hear what only you can share, see what only you can show, and experience what only you can take them through.

As you continue to develop your Powerful Presence, time and circumstances will bring you together—exactly as time and circumstances have brought you and me together. Until that time, I wish you every illumination on your Journey. I hope our paths cross again.

Dance into Your Power

Epilogue

The Journey to Powerful Presence is the Journey to *yourself*—the source of your power.

Now that you've taken this Journey, you've experienced things you might never have otherwise. You're a resource for yourself as well as for others. You can build on everything you've learned here to dance into your power for the rest of your life.

Writing this book has confirmed for me that everything you discover about yourself is enriched with use. The more you use your strengths, the more powerful they become. The more you trust yourself, the more comfortable you become in your own skin. And the more you use your strengths in your relationships with other people, the more magical your world becomes. Dancing becomes your instinct.

As I was putting together the material for this book, I came across something I'd written in my leadership training in 2004–2005 (the training that required me to use my inner lion to climb a redwood tree on the ropes course). We had to write a statement about what we'd discovered about ourselves in the year we'd spent in the training. It was astonishing to read; it's only clear to me now that it predicts my work with Powerful Presence as well as this book. Here's what I wrote:

I have the ability to see into the heart of things, past appearances, to what is really real. I can almost reach in and touch it.

I am at my most powerful when I speak what I have seen and touched in a clear and calm way to illuminate it for others.

That statement captured my understanding of myself eight years ago. Even though I identified something powerful inside me, I still didn't quite know what to do with it. You may have had a similar experience doing the exercises in this book.

Creating the Journey to Powerful Presence as a course—and in this book—required my willingness to keep traveling so I could discover the meaning of what I found. I hope you'll keep traveling, too.

I hope this book has inspired you to look into yourself to find the treasure that lies within you. Now that you're on it, your Journey can last as long as your lifetime. Now that you have the distinctions, structures, and strategies to get you started, I have no doubt that you'll be able to create more of your own. The world will be richer when you do.

As we conclude our Journey together, I'd like to leave you with a final story. I wrote it in 1996 as the epilogue of my second book, *Pizza and the Art of Life Management*, which captured my program called *Stress Arresters*—just like this book captures my program called *The Journey to Powerful Presence*.

Stress Arresters changed my life and brought Chuck Beatty to me. It captured my understanding of the distinctions, structures, and strategies for managing your life that I'd learned in my work as a substance abuse counselor.

Sixteen years ago, as I was writing this story for my epilogue, I had no idea where it and *Pizza and the Art of Life Management* would lead me. As I look at it again, I can see that it led me straight to this book—and to you.

This story makes it clear to me that there has been a pattern to my life that has guided me on my Journey. I believe that I'm no different from anyone else; there's a pattern to everyone's life. Once you discover the pattern in yours, you will discover the road that takes you directly to your purpose in life. My hope is that you will see what I mean when you read the story.

I call this story …

The Faerie Queen

Once upon a time, there was a little girl who knew she was a Faerie Princess.

She would drape herself in her mother's old sheets and float around the house, practicing being regal. In her mind's eye, those sheets were garments of the finest silk. She could feel, emerging from between her little shoulders, the most beautiful gossamer wings made of the most delicate of colors.

She would tie long braids of yarn to her head, remembering that she had hair that flowed down her back past her knees. She'd put flowers in her yarn hair, remembering that her Faerie hair was bound in the brightest of jewels and the whitest of freshwater pearls. She was a Faerie Princess, after all, and she could have all the jewels in the Universe.

At night she would look up at the stars in the sky and wish on the first one she saw. She thought great thoughts—about the world and her place in it and about all the wonderful things she would do when she grew up and became the Faerie Queen.

She loved the fireflies on summer nights, seashells and the sound of the ocean, big fires in winter, and laughing. Most of all, she loved *life*. If she could have, she would have gulped it from a glass.

Then one day, an evil sorcerer put a very deep, very wide, and very strong spell on the little Princess. As a result, she completely forgot who she was.

Because of this spell, she became convinced that she was merely a mortal girl, and not a very pretty one at that. She lost her beautiful hair and all the jewels and pearls that bound it. She lost her gossamer wings and her resplendent silken clothes.

All she had now were shabby clothes that didn't fit. Her hair never grew past her ears, which were always dirty. She never floated anywhere, either. Once the spell had been cast on her, she kept her eyes and head down and never looked at the stars.

As she continued to grow up, she went to school and (mostly) did as she was told. She didn't laugh much.

As she grew older, she simply wandered through her life. She met people, did things, moved, and worked, but she never remembered who she really was.

∞

When she was a quarter century old, something mysterious happened. It happened at a time when all she wanted to do was die. She had been so miserable for so long that she could not imagine living long enough to turn thirty. However, try as she might, she simply couldn't come up with a decent method of killing herself. There just wasn't anything available that she could manage to use successfully.

One day, in the midst of her distress, she heard about a woman who was helping people find their true spirits to align themselves with their purpose in life. She figured that it wasn't possible that she could be one of the people who had a purpose in life. Since she couldn't go on being miserable, and she couldn't figure out a way to end her life, she thought the woman might be able to suggest something that could help her, even if it was just a little.

So she went to see the woman, whose name, by the way, was Nutmeg. When this girl, who was born a Faerie Princess and had grown up without remembering it, arrived at Nutmeg's door, she was welcomed graciously by Nutmeg herself. "Come in, My Dear," said Nutmeg. "You are welcome here."

At this kindness from Nutmeg, the grown-up girl realized that she was, all of a sudden, uncomfortable. As a matter of fact, she realized that she felt ashamed to be receiving such kindness from a stranger. She thought to herself, "If only Nutmeg knew what an awful, unworthy creature I am, she would never be so nice to me. I don't deserve this." But she went in anyway.

Once she was inside, Nutmeg offered her a cup of hot tea, which she accepted without looking up. Then, sure enough, just the way she'd heard it would happen, Nutmeg asked her if she had come about a mirror. Looking into her teacup, the grown-up girl said, "If you've got a spare one that nobody else wants. Yes, please."

After looking at the grown-up girl with the most tender smile imaginable, Nutmeg explained about the mirrors. "Every one of these mirrors was created in such a way that whoever looks into them will see her true self—no matter how she appears to others or to herself in any other mirror. It just so happens," continued Nutmeg, "that no one who has ever looked into one of these mirrors has ever seen anything less than a beautiful, magical creature, full of Light and love, looking back."

The grown-up girl said to herself, "Well there's always a first time." And then, as desperate and ashamed as she was, she looked in the mirror.

At that exact moment, she had the strongest physical sensation she had ever experienced. She felt as if she were being held, like a little baby bird, in the great kind hands of some Being much greater than her—much greater than the world, even. She was held so tenderly, so gently, that it almost made her heart break with emotion.

As she looked into the mirror, she saw the most beautiful face she had ever seen in her life. Here were the warmest, brightest, most gentle eyes. This face looking back at her had radiant skin, a warm smile—and dimples!

She heard, with every fiber of her being, the most tender, sweetest voice say to her, "You are beautiful. You are good. You are a child of God, and *you are immeasurably loved.*

For a few exquisite moments, the grown-up girl was completely filled with Light. It was the most amazing, healing, peaceful feeling that she had ever known. For those few moments, she was filled with something that can only be described as delight.

If she had died right there on the spot, she would have gotten her dearest wish—she would have died in bliss.

∞

Despite her dearest wish, however, the grown-up girl did not die. In fact, she started to live. From that day forward, she searched the entire world to find something that would connect her to that feeling of delight—that feeling of complete peacefulness she had experienced when she looked into that mirror.

Although she began her search immediately, she did not find it right away. The time she spent searching is of little importance to our story; what matters is that she searched as long as she had to. She never stopped until she found what she sought, even though it seemed like a very long time.

It appeared to her, during the years that she searched, that she was having little success. In truth, though, every single thing she did had a negative effect on the sorcerer's spell. Bit by bit, it was being dismantled. Bit by bit, it was losing its power over her.

However, since it was a very strong spell (as well as very wide and deep), it took some time for her efforts to show. After a while, though, it became obvious—even to her—that something was, in fact, changing inside of her.

After that, it was not long before she started to take better care of herself. She started to get more rest and pay attention to what she ate (especially breakfast). She started to walk in the parks around her home. For the first time in a very long time, she noticed how beautiful the trees were, how graceful the birds that flew over her head were, and, in summer, beginning at dusk, how many fireflies there were.

The fireflies reminded her of the stars; soon she began to look for them every night. Once or twice, she even wished on the first one she saw. The beauty of the stars made her sigh with happiness.

Looking around and listening to the sounds of a world that was becoming more and more beautiful to her made her feel so relaxed and peaceful that it was almost like that feeling she had looking into that mirror all those years ago. Breathing slowly and deeply, she found that she could keep that feeling longer, so she began to breathe that way whenever she thought about it.

If the world was becoming more beautiful, so was that grown-up girl. (One day she even thought she felt the touch of gossamer wings brush by her cheek.)

Over the years, as she continued to grow, she noticed that there were times when she felt completely free of that old sorcerer's spell. She started talking to herself in a gentle, loving way. On the occasions when she did this, she felt certain that the old spells had no power over her.

She looked for the positive people, places, and things in the world. And when she was with them or near them, she had the strongest feeling of delight—just as she had when she first looked into that mirror.

As the years continued to pass, she couldn't help smiling when she thought of all the growing up she had done and how far out of the clutches of the sorcerer's spell she had come.

∞

One day, while she was out with some friends sharing her favorite pizza, she happened to look into the mirror that hung along the wall behind their table. There, looking out at her from within that mirror, was the most beautiful Faerie Queen that she had ever seen—or could ever have imagined! She was breathtakingly beautiful. She had the longest, shiniest hair; the brightest, most sparkling eyes; and a laughing, dimpled face. In her hair, which was bound with ropes of the most opalescent freshwater pearls, she wore jewels that caught the light and flashed with gemfire. Her robes were of the finest cobalt silk, with a swath of sparkling, silvery stars at her collar and wrists—and she had the most magnificent pair of luminous, gossamer wings.

The grown-up girl could not stop looking at the Faerie Queen in the mirror. After a moment, though, the Faerie Queen winked at the grown-up girl and disappeared with a smile.

Everyone at the table was looking at the grown-up girl with concern. "Are you OK?" asked her best friend, who was sitting right next to her. "All of a sudden, you were somewhere else!"

"Yes, I guess I was," said the grown-up girl with a smile. That's all she would say about what happened. She was smiling because she had decided in that very moment, as she was sharing her favorite pizza with her dear friends, that she would spend more time with herself, every day. She would make it a daily practice to look into the mirror—and she would meet the Faerie Queen again.

So every day, she did just that.

With all that focus and attention, it didn't take long for the Faerie Queen to take up residence in the grown-up girl's bathroom mirror. And every day, they spent time with each other.

The more time they spent together, the weaker all the parts of the sorcerer's spell became. Pretty soon, it seemed to have disappeared altogether.

∽

Day by day, the grown-up girl began to discover things that she really wanted to do—and she did them. She made new friends, had more experiences, and even (much to her delight!) found that she was one of those people who have a purpose in life. She even discovered that *there were people in this world who thought that she was a delight.*

To her great joy, she met the love of her life. Every day, she continued to build a life of her own choosing, with love to share. And share it she did, with all she met.

∽

One day, years later, as she was looking into her bathroom mirror at the Faerie Queen, she noticed that her own hair seemed very long—heavy, even. She put her hand in it and found a cord of freshwater pearls and jewels—and hair that flowed past her knees.

She glanced at her wrists and noticed the cuffs of her cobalt silken robe were made of silvery, sparkling stars. She looked down at her feet and saw that her beautiful robes reached the floor and spread out around her, covering her feet. She reached over her shoulders and touched them—the most resplendent pair of luminous, gossamer wings!

The girl who had been a Faerie Princess, who had grown up without remembering who she was, had discovered (much to her delight and astonishment!) that she had become the Faerie Queen—the most beautiful, the most worthy, the most thankful one on the planet.

And since she was the Faerie Queen, she could create anything she desired in the Universe.

And that's exactly what she did.

∽

Now I can tell you that everything you just read is true.

The Faerie Queen is the real story of my Journey to Powerful Presence; you probably recognized Gwen playing the part of Nutmeg.

Thank you for sharing this Journey with me. Your story is out there waiting for you to find it. And, just like Nutmeg, I have every confidence that you will.

Acknowledgements

A Journey like this is the result of connecting to a community of people whose impact is so great it simply can't be measured. There's a multitude of people I want to thank here. Due to space, many must go unnamed. Whether or not I mention you, I hope you know who you are—and how much I treasure you.

Special thanks go to these champions, inspirers, and instigators:

Without my late parents, Dr. D.A. and M. Eileen Connolly Drennen, there would be no Journey. They gave me life—and provided me with the intellectual, emotional, spiritual, and physical "roots and soil" I needed to fulfill my destiny. Although our journey together wasn't always easy or smooth, I'm proud to be their daughter. What lives on inside me is their love for me and their desire for my success.

Without my sisters and brother, Deirdre, Susan, Eileen, Don, and Beth, I would have missed out on so many experiences that helped me grow. Each of them has claimed their own Journey and is living it to the fullest in his or her own way. I'm so thankful for what each of them has contributed to my life.

My Journey to Powerful Presence would not have begun on the day that it did without the courageous support of my *Irish twin*, Deirdre Marie Drennen. On my way out of the house that day, I told her what I was doing and asked her to give me fifteen minutes lead time before delivering my farewell note to our parents. She gave me that lead time, which allowed me to successfully disappear. She withstood the firestorm that ensued after she took my message to my parents in a note that began, "Dear Sir and Madam." Although it was my belief that our relationship had deteriorated past the point of being parents and child, and my message was meant to let them off the hook in their relationship with me, this was not its impact. Deirdre faced my parents alone and bore the brunt of my father's rage and my mother's shock. I can't imagine how difficult that evening must have been for her as she paid the price for my freedom. Not a moment has passed that I have not appreciated the gift she gave me that night and the treasure she is, and always has been, in my life.

Before I found the teachers and mentors who would help me embark on this Journey, a handful of people took me under their wings and protected me so I could safely reach the start of my road:

- In my family: my maternal grandparents, John P. and Helen R. Connolly, my Papa and Nana. Their love and attention nourished me at a time when I needed it most. It gave me resilience and resourcefulness that I tapped in to for many years until I could create that kind of love and attention for myself.

- My teachers: Mrs. Beaudette; Sister Mary Agathine, OP; Sister Mary Monica, OP; Father Timone; and (Marist) Brother Simeon. Although school was normally trying for me, each of these teachers saw an ember of light in me and fanned it. They kept me going despite the challenges of undiagnosed ADHD. They gave me a reason to connect with what they were teaching. They left me with an experience of the power of Attention.

- Others who saw something in me worth nourishing, even when I didn't: Ken Baron, John and Mary Baron, Joe Luna, Matilde Goldwitz, Dennis Kinlaw, Barbara Smith, George Gochenaur, and David Michael Martin, BMC.

Gwen Nichols saved my life. She taught me the first distinctions, structures, and strategies that helped me find my way to my destiny. No words can adequately describe my gratitude to her. After we completed our work together in 1978, I never saw her again. My hope is that her work with me will live on forever—in the pages of this book and on the Journeys that each Dancer takes because of it.

Mary Lou Holt was my therapist in the mid-1980s, and her husband, Dan Adams, was my clinical supervisor for substance abuse counseling at about the same time. Working with them continued my education in the distinctions, structures, and strategies to which Gwen had introduced me. Our work together was instrumental in my learning to plot the course of my life and in my being willing to take the action required to do so. My debt to them is as huge as my love for them.

My instructors and colleagues in the recovery field, and the clients I worked with in my eight years as a certified substance abuse counselor in California, Florida, and Texas, gave me real-world skills and inspired in me a passion for transformation. They helped me build a practice of distinctions, structures, and strategies that I still use today.

Richard Bandler and John Grinder took me from Kansas to Oz in 1984 when I was introduced to their book, *Frogs into Princes*. Once I experienced the magic of NLP, there was no going back to an ordinary life. NLP was the fast train that sped me on my way to creating both the life I have today and the Journey to Powerful Presence. I've never seen anything like it for instant and long-lasting transformation. You'll find NLP distinctions, structures, and strategies in everything I do.

The late John Wilson, PhD, was the most exceptional teacher I've ever seen. So much of who I am in the classroom was inspired by the transformative experience I had as his student. He was the epitome of Powerful Presence.

My three dearest friends, Barbara, Maggie, and Rhea, have given me countless opportunities over the last thirty-nine years to redefine my notion of family and practice what I'm discovering in the learning lab of our friendship. I will forever be indebted to each of them.

Starting in 1990, the colleagues and friends I made from my memberships in the National Speaker's Association, Meeting Professionals International, and the International Coach Federation, and my training with the Coaches Training Institute, have given me a treasure trove of experiences that have supported my Powerful Presence. I can't imagine how I could possibly have gotten a more thorough real-world education. Thank you, all of you—and you know who you are.

Maggie and the late Al Beatty gave me a home that was every bit as nourishing as the one I experienced with my Papa and Nanny. Ever committed to caring for their children in the most powerful and dynamic of ways, they even invited Chuck (their oldest son) and me to live with them "for a few months" to get our feet on the ground after our inadvertent move to the area. That few months turned into eighteen—we left their home by moving into a newly built home of our own. Although I was very hesitant to move in with them because of my history, I soon realized that I had stumbled into the kind of family I'd been looking for all my life. Thank you, Mom and Dad—for everything!

My dance teachers transformed my presence and gave lift to my gossamer wings. Pierre Dulaine, whom I met in the movies *Mad Hot Ballroom* and *Take the Lead*, opened my mind to the possibility that I could dance and gave me a hunger to try. Ameenah, owner of Visions of the Nile in Akron, Ohio, with whom I took private lessons, helped me identify the six dance moves that are natural for my body, which I now employ in every dance. Julie Buckeye, owner of World of Dances in Cuyahoga Falls, Ohio, taught me in her lively classes that no one can dance like I can, and gave me the book *Grandmother's Secrets: The Ancient Rituals and Healing Power of Belly Dancing*. Jennifer Leslie MacDonald, owner of Martell School of Dance in Akron, Ohio, was the first dancer to identify me as a "natural performer" and illuminate for me just how much of a dancer I am and always have been. And Tara Tober, Artistic Director at Contact Dance Academy in Akron, Ohio, who introduced me to the American Dance Therapy Association and pointed me to the connections between dance therapy and dancing into your power with Powerful Presence.

The first Dancers on the Journey to Powerful Presence in the September 2009 teleclass taught me more than they will ever know. At the time I had no idea whether my distinctions, structures, and strategies would be transferrable; this class showed me that they were. For twelve weeks, they played full-out to make every discovery they could. They started out as strangers in three different states, and created community very quickly. Their willingness to trust the Journey put Powerful Presence on the map. Thank you, Dawn, Pam, Patty, Sharon, and Shirley.

As a result of the discoveries we made in that first teleclass, I began the process that resulted in this book in January of 2010. Although it took me exactly two years to find it, all the Dancers in the intervening classes and those who read my early drafts were instrumental in helping me find the perfect voice with which to share this Journey. Thank you all!

The Powerful Presence Community that began with that teleclass has grown in leaps and bounds over the last three years. It's proved to me that developing Powerful Presence is something that makes a difference in people's lives. It's been a pleasure and a privilege to work with each of the Dancers in the classes and teleclasses—and in the advanced classes and teleclasses. More people are learning about Powerful Presence at the monthly luncheons that began in September of 2010. I believe that Gwen would be very proud to see it.

As the Powerful Presence Community has grown, it's grown past my ability to handle all the details of coordinating the classes and luncheons as well as my writing, speaking, training, and coaching clients. Since April of 2011, my spectacular VA, Pam Ryan, CEO of Virtual Ringmaster, LLC, has been taking care of those details and making me wonder how I ever did business without her. Thank you, Pam—you astound and delight me daily.

The name Gwen always connects me to Gwen Nichols and her alter ego, Nutmeg. How perfect is it that my editor at Love Your Life Publishing is also named Gwen! Thank you for your rigorous attention to every detail and for helping me polish my words to a shine.

There is one person who saw the dream of this book coming true before I did: my publisher, Lynne Klippel. We both agree that fate put us together. We met in a very long line at a Starbucks at the 2007 International Coach Federation Conference in St. Louis. We spoke for twenty minutes; we had instant rapport and then went our separate ways after exchanging contact info. Over the next several years, we kept up by phone and email. While I was in the midst of writing the drafts that would finally lead to this book, I told Lynne that I was frustrated about not being able to find a way to share this Journey. She was so calm. She told me that "no book comes before its time" and that "great books are just like great bottles of wine—they take a while to ferment." Her comments helped me get through the next year of writing until I broke the code and found my voice in January of 2012. Once that happened, the writing flowed as easily as pouring a glass of wine. For the last two years, Lynne has been the biggest champion of this book. Her support has been instrumental in bringing you what you hold in your hands. Thank you, Lynne, with all of my heart.

And finally, there's nothing in my awesome life today that hasn't been touched by the experience of being treasured and nurtured by Chuck Beatty, the Love of My Life, for over twenty-two years. When he told me that I should do my dream and let him help me, truer words were never spoken to describe this journey we're taking together. This book would not be possible without his masterful layout and insightful editing. With tender and skillful coaching, he helped me bring the best of myself to each page. And his cover design takes my breath away! There are no words to adequately describe my gratitude, joy, and amazement at the gift of this remarkable man in my life. Fortunately, the look between us says it all. ILYAF! YON.

Dance into Your Power

Powerful Presence Resources

The Books That Shaped My Journey and Deepened My Learning

Reading has been a passion of mine since I learned to read at age six; it's always been a great source of learning for me, especially when I had no other teachers or mentors. I have to admit I'm voracious about it! There are so many books that have helped me on my way that I've forgotten more titles than I can count.

There are some books that I will never forget and never let go of; they've had such a profound effect on me that I will keep them forever. The books on the list below are those kinds of books. If you're looking for a window into the ideas that helped me formulate the distinctions, structures, and strategies of Powerful Presence, these books will give you a great start.

I. Early books: my first teachers and role models

William S. Baring-Gould, Editor: *The Annotated Sherlock Holmes*

Ram Das: *Be Here Now*

Viktor Frankl: *Man's Search for Meaning*

Louise L. Hay: *You Can Heal Your Life*

Richard Hittleman: *Richard Hittleman's Yoga: 28 Day Exercise Plan*

C.S. Lewis: *Till We Have Faces*

J. R. R. Tolkien: *The Lord of the Rings*

II. Books that helped me on my way

Richard Bandler and John Grinder: *Frogs into Princes*

Madelyn Burley-Allen: *Listening: The Forgotten Skill*

Richard Bach: *Illusions*

Joseph Campbell: *The Hero with a Thousand Faces*

Joseph Campbell with Bill Moyers: *The Power of Myth*

James Hillman: *The Soul's Code*

Rokelle Lerner: *Affirmations for Adult Children of Alcoholics*

Dan Millman: *The Way of the Peaceful Warrior*

Thomas Moore: *Care of the Soul*

Clarissa Pinkola Estes, PhD: *Women Who Run with the Wolves*

Bill Plotkin: *Soulcraft*

Jean Shinoda-Bolen: *Goddesses in Every Woman*

Bill Watterson: *There's Treasure Everywhere* (and all the Calvin and Hobbes books)

Marianne Williamson: *Return to Love*

Gary Zukav: *The Seat of the Soul*

III. Books that continue the message of Powerful Presence and deepen my learning

Rosina-Fawzia Al-Rawi and Monique Arav: *Grandmothers Secrets: The Ancient Rituals and Healing Power of Belly Dancing*

Richard Bandler: *Get the Life You Want*

His Holiness the Dalai Lama: *The Art of Happiness*

Warren Grossman: *To Be Healed by the Earth*

Peter Senge, C. Otto Scharmer, Joseph Jaworski and Betty Sue Flowers: *Presence: An Exploration of Profound Change in People, Organizations and Society*

Marci Shimoff: *Love for No Reason*

Kathleen Ragan: *Fearless Girls, Wise Women and Beloved Sisters*

Dance into Your Power

About The Author

Maia Beatty is *The Powerful Presence Trainer and Coach* and the principal of *Discover Your Powerful Presence*, a division of Maia Beatty & Associates, Inc., in Akron, Ohio.

Her mission is to help people identify, access, and claim their Powerful Presence.

Maia is the creator of over forty motivational keynote presentations and learner-focused, performance-based training programs, including the twelve-week program: *Dance into Your Power on the Journey to Powerful Presence*, the six-week *Advanced Classes*, and *PowerSpeak!: The Art & Science of Confident Speaking*.

She is a Master Trainer. Maia has been training adults since 1982, and training trainers since 1999, across the US as well as in Canada, the UK and Australia. Her specialty is providing the environment that allows her learners to identify, access, and use their incomparable power so they can increase their skills and apply what they learn immediately.

Maia is an international keynote speaker who has been using her warm and inspiring style since 1987 to connect her audiences with their own Powerful Presence and authentic self. She has spoken across the US and Canada, as well as in the UK and the Dominican Republic.

She is a speaking coach. With her original program, *PowerSpeak!*, Maia has had a 100 percent success rate in increasing the speaking confidence and skill of her clients since 1999. She is also a co-active coach, helping her clients transform their circumstances and develop their unique Powerful Presence since 2004.

Maia has a BA in psychology from Texas A&M, Corpus Christi. She is an NLP practitioner and a graduate of the Coaches Training Institute, with certificates in coaching, business development, and leadership. She is a veteran of the U.S. Navy.

Maia is the winner of the 2011 Connector's Choice Award for "Best Speaker/Facilitator in Northeast Ohio."

She lives in Bath, Ohio, with her beloved husband, Chuck Beatty, and their two eccentric cats, Fionn mac Cumhaill (McCool) and Isis Marie.

Maia is currently working on her next book.

You can find more information about Maia and her classes at *www.maiabeatty.com.*